Using Assessments to Teach for Understanding

A CASEBOOK FOR EDUCATORS

Using Assessments to Teach for Understanding

A CASEBOOK FOR EDUCATORS

Editors

Judith H. Shulman
West Ed

Andrea Whittaker
San Jose State University

Michele Lew
The Carnegie Foundation for the Advancement of Teaching

FOREWORD BY SUZANNE M. WILSON

Teachers College, Columbia University
New York and London

This document is supported by funds from the National Partnership for Excellence and Accountability in Teaching (NPEAT), as well as from the U.S. Department of Education, Office of Educational Research and Improvement, contract number ED-01-CO-0012. The interpretations and opinions expressed are those of the authors and editors, and do not necessarily reflect the views or policies of NPEAT or the Department of Education.

Published by Teachers College Press, 1234 Amsterdam Avenue, New York, NY 10027

Library of Congress Cataloging-in-Publication Data

Using assessments to teach for understanding : a casebook for educators / editors Judith H. Shulman, Andrea Whittaker, Michele Lew.
     p. cm.
  Includes bibliographical references (p.   ) and index.
  ISBN 0-8077-4214-7 (pbk. : alk. paper)
    1. Educational tests and measurements—Case studies. 2. Education—Evaluation—Case studies. I. Shulman, Judith. II. Whittaker, Andrea (Andrea Kay). III. Lew, Michele.
LB3051 .U86 2002
371.36—dc21   2001055686

ISBN 0-8077-4214-7 (paper)

Printed on acid-free paper
Manufactured in the United States of America

09 08 07 06 05 04 03 02   8 7 6 5 4 3 2 1

Contents

CHAPTER 6
Working with Case Writers: A Methodological Note   123

Foreword

In the past 15 years, cases have enjoyed a surge in popularity. Their attraction seems obvious, for who doesn't like a good story? And the stories contained in this volume are good. The authors pull us into their classrooms, and introduce us to the wonders and challenges of working with children. We worry for Alicia, a boisterous and courageous child, as she struggles to conquer coordinate geometry. We smile with recognition as Esteban's teacher reports on her struggles to teach him how to write his own paragraphs, rather than paraphrase those offered as models. We empathize with teacher authors who simultaneously must respond to new curricular mandates while also paying attention to the needs of their individual students. The details of school and life among children come alive. We remember how tender children are, how hard it is to teach math, how overwhelming the tidal wave of new educational policies can feel. Like other good stories, these cases transport us to other places and times. They remind us of places we have been, people we have known.

But we do the authors and users of cases a disservice if we presume that cases are simply good story-telling. This collection of cases represents much more than that. Shulman has often urged those of us interested in cases to ask ourselves the question, "What is this a case of?" For rich cases, there are multiple answers to that question. This casebook is no different, for I can think of many answers to the question, "What is this casebook a case of?" Here I suggest two.

One answer would focus on teachers and their knowledge. Teachers have long noted that some research seems disconnected from practice. This disconnect is compounded by the fact that other scholars have also noted that there is only spotty scholarship available on teaching. That is, while teaching is a widespread practice in K–12 schools and universities, teachers seldom make public what they have learned through their practice. Furthermore, few forums exist in which teachers can then present what they think they have learned for public review by peers. I might think I know a lot about teaching third-grade social studies, or about the use of assessment in teaching sixth-grade science, but without professional forums for presenting my ideas, those ideas remain my own, never critiqued or tested by peers. Thus, there is no legacy, no reliable documentation of the practical knowledge that teachers acquire over time. New generations of teachers are left to create their own understanding, rather than building on the experience accumulated across generations.

Why don't we have a robust scholarship of teaching? There are many answers to that question. One concerns how knowledge is held. Jerome Bruner once made a distinction between paradigmatic and narrative ways of knowing. At the risk of oversimplifying his argument, he claimed that we hold knowledge in two distinct ways. Some knowledge is held in the form of principles. That knowledge is detachable from the process that led to its creation. Other knowledge we hold in narratives, stories. One cannot detach such knowledge from its process, for the knowledge is in the narrative, not in some singular, simple moral that comes at the end of a story.

Teaching knowledge comes in both forms. Some things we know in the form of principles; wait time, for example, is a detachable principle that I can use as a teacher across multiple contexts. Other teaching knowledge, however, can only be held in story form, it can't be reduced to a simple solution. Such knowledge does not fit the social science paradigm that dominated research on teaching for so long: Social scientists often want principles. They believe, like other scientists, in paradigmatic knowledge. But teachers know that principles alone do not inform good teaching. Like lawyers, teachers also reason by analogy, comparing one case to another, looking for similarities, considering contextual clues, and acknowledging the situated aspects of teaching.

This form of teaching knowledge—situated, rich, detailed narrative—has been more elusive. These cases—and others written by K–12 and university teachers and leaders—begin to address that void. These are not simply good stories: they are teaching knowledge, a scholarship of teaching. Tested through peer review and revision, these cases leave a legacy for teachers of future generations to use as they reason case by case.

There is another way to answer the question, "What is this casebook a case of?" This not the first casebook to come from researchers at WestEd, for as the editors of the volume note, WestEd's Institute for Case Development has a 15-year history of helping teachers make their knowledge public. And so this casebook is also a case of a *method*: case-writing. The editors have built upon the experiences of other editors, developing and refining a practice for helping teachers write and rewrite, discuss and critique cases.

This case-writing is, in effect, a *pedagogy* of professional development. Thus, teacher educators and teacher leaders can learn much about how to help teachers learn as they read these cases. Chapter 6 contains a detailed description of the process that the editors used to enable the development of these cases. In her methodological note, Judith Shulman walks us through both the stages of that process, and the reasons for those stages. The facilitator's guide adds another layer to the casebook, for it helps the user of the cases think through the substantive and pedagogical issues associated with the use of cases. This explicit attention to the pedagogy of case development and case use is a much-needed addition to the literature on cases and their use in teacher education and professional development.

When I was a child, I loved good stories. I still do. But I find myself drawn especially to good stories that are anchored in larger issues. This casebook represents larger educational issues faced by all educators. The cases constitute a scholarship of teaching: readers will cull from them important ideas about what children find difficult, the challenges that arise with the use of assessments, and the options teachers have in integrating assessments into their practice. The casebook also presents a pedagogy of professional development. It teaches us much about how to help teachers learn from and in their practice. I encourage you to read and use these cases. They left me eager to return to my own teaching, armed with a new practice and new insights into students and assessments, learning and teaching.

Suzanne M. Wilson
Michigan State University

Preface

The recent standards movement presents today's teachers with unprecedented challenges. Achieving higher academic standards for all students depends not just on a thorough knowledge of pedagogical content, but on teachers' ability to tell what students really know and can do and where the learning gaps are so they can target instruction to fill those gaps. Yet studies and experience show that most teachers lack this "assessment literacy." Many feel sorely unprepared to interpret state standards through their own instructional practice, to design their own classroom assessments, and to use a variety of performance data not just to *measure* but to *improve* student learning. This casebook, initiated under a grant from the National Partnership for Excellence and Accountability in Teaching, focuses directly on these challenges.

Written by new and veteran teachers, these narratives fill a glaring gap in the case literature, as they portray the challenges, celebrations, and dilemmas that all teachers face in meeting the standards-based requirements mandated by their districts and state departments. All of the cases have gone through a series of iterative drafts and have been field-tested with new and veteran teachers. The insights we gained from these experiences have been compiled into a facilitator's guide, which accompanies this edition in a separate volume.

This collection of cases is part of a nationwide effort to capture and use practitioner knowledge to better prepare teachers for the reality of today's classrooms. Unlike business, law, and medicine, education has been slower to make formal use of cases as professional training tools. But interest in case-based teaching is now growing in both teacher preparation and ongoing professional development programs. This growing interest began during the 1980s reform movement as it became increasingly clear that many teachers are unprepared for the huge array of challenges presented by a student population and workplace vastly different from previous ones. Novices often find the gritty, real-life classroom to be light-years from the ideal they had imagined as students. Spotlighting this gap between theory and practice, the 1986 Carnegie report, *A Nation Prepared: Teachers for the Twenty-First Century*, recommended that teacher preparation institutions use "cases illustrating a great variety of teaching problems" as "a major focus of instruction" (p. 76).

What do we mean by "case"? Cases are candid, dramatic, highly readable accounts of teaching events or a series of events. They offer a problem-based snapshot of an on-the-job dilemma. Read on one's own, cases offer the vicarious experience of walking in another's shoes. In group discussion, they are especially powerful, allowing differing points of view to be aired and examined. For that reason, cases are consciously designed to provoke discussion that is engaging, demanding, and intellectually exciting. While some cases are written by researchers, those we have pioneered over the past fifteen years at WestEd's Institute for Case Development are crafted by teachers themselves. Because they tell vivid, moving stories, cases give life to abstract principles and propositions, and are likely to be remembered. Teacher educators, administrators, mentors, and staff developers use cases to trigger discussion about why a given strategy works or does not work.

As they discuss the cases in this book, beginners can learn to use assessment to plan instruction and to examine rubrics and benchmarks to see if they appropriately promote student learning. They also learn to frame problems from multiple perspectives, interpret complex situations, and identify decision points and reflect on possible consequences—that is, they learn to think like teachers.

Veterans discuss teaching situations that mirror their own, in the process reflecting on their values, attitudes, assumptions, and teaching strategies, and wrestling with the disequilibrium this creates. As a result, they often change or broaden their beliefs about teaching and learning and thus adopt very different ways of working with students.

WESTED'S APPROACH

The WestEd case-writing process makes practitioners themselves the subjects, producers, and consumers of action research. We emphasize this because teachers generally have few mechanisms for recording and preserving their accumulated knowledge. When a teacher retires or leaves the profession, her understanding, methods, and materials—which should form a legacy to the profession, the community, and the school—are generally lost. Today, however, there is an expanding literature on the practitioner experience. WestEd's Casebooks contribute to it by combining the growing body of research about teaching with specific accounts of classroom dilemmas written by teachers themselves.

Cases are not simply narrative descriptions of events. To call something a case is to make a theoretical claim—that it is a case *of* something, or an instance of a larger class. This is not to say that all cases illustrate, exemplify, or teach a theoretical principle. To be valuable as a case, however, the narrative should be representative of a class or type of dilemma, problem, or quandary that arises with some frequency in teaching situations. Most rich cases are cases "of" many things. Cases may also be exemplars of principles, describing by their detail a general pattern of practice.

ABOUT THIS CASEBOOK

These 15 cases were written in collaboration with two teacher networks: 1) Joint Venture: Silicon Valley Network, a nonprofit organization that brings together education, business, and civic leaders to improve the Silicon Valley's economy and quality of life; and 2) the New Teacher Cen-

ter, University of California, Santa Cruz. The teachers in these networks meet regularly—sometimes in school teams, sometimes as individuals—to discuss the challenges of their experiences and learn from one another. They all come with a focus on improving student learning in literacy, mathematics, or science, and all of them teach in standards-based environments.

Most of the teacher-authors teach in diverse, low-income schools, many of which are located in rural, predominantly Latino areas in the mid-coastal region of California. A few also teach in the suburban areas of Silicon Valley. But all are passionately committed to meeting the needs of their students and finding ways to improve performance. And they spend hours grappling with methods that satisfy both state and district mandates as well as their own theories, philosophies, and intuitions about good educational practices. Much of this activity is directed toward discovering effective approaches to multiple forms of assessment; the teachers are energized by their commitment to guide appropriate instruction for all students. Some have used performance assessments and scored them with rubrics for several years, while others—novices as well as veterans—are learning to use them for the first time. Yet whatever the experience, all would agree that creating and using these assessments effectively requires much more time, energy, and commitment than more traditional approaches.

To stimulate analysis and reflection, all of the cases are problem-focused and deal with issues that the writers hoped would be relevant to others' experience. As you will note when you read the cases, they embed questions around dilemmas that involve:

- examining the use of assessments that guide appropriate instruction
- questioning the role of assessment in the learning process, especially for special needs students
- exploring the use of assessments to promote self-efficacy
- creating and using rubrics that appropriately score student work
- converting assessment data to equitable and fair grades

- analyzing the use of retention and/or social promotion policies to increase student learning
- examining the impact of high-stakes assessment on the social/emotional and learning needs of children
- using state and district benchmarks that may be counterproductive for English language learners
- coping with time demands of increased assessment procedures
- dealing with alignment problems between district and state assessments
- reporting assessment results to families and other stakeholders

We have tried to sequence the cases to highlight these dilemmas. But since cases are usually "of" many things, they often don't fit neatly in any one chapter or section. An analysis that examines how individual assessment dilemmas are portrayed across the cases is presented in Table I.1 in the Introduction.

Three of the cases are written by teacher advisors from the New Teacher Project, who focus on supporting new teachers. Their cases can be used as professional development tools by other advisors (see the Introduction to Chapter 5 by Ellen Moir, director of this program, for more information about the teacher advisors).

For those interested in pursuing additional reading about assessment, an Annotated Bibliography is offered at the end of this volume. And if you are interested in adapting our case development process to create your own set of cases, methodological notes and "Guidelines for Writing Cases" (see Appendix A) are also offered at the end of the volume.

TIPS FOR USING THESE CASES

Cases are powerful discussion catalysts. Good discussion can help people dig into a case and learn things that help them think differently about such issues as planning curriculum, instructional methods, student needs, equity, assessment, and so forth (see Lundeberg, Levin, & Harrington, 1999, for a review of the literature on what can be gained from case discussion).

As you read these cases, you may want to ask yourself questions such as: How did the teacher frame the problems he or she encountered? In what other ways could the problem have been framed? What did this teacher actually do and why? With what result? What alternative strategies might have been tried? At what risk? With what consequences? What were students thinking and feeling? How did they try to communicate this to the teacher? How does this teacher's story parallel experiences of your own? How might this case (or case discussion) lead you to think of different ways of dealing with these dilemmas? What principles of teaching and learning can be generated from your analysis? Deliberations stimulated from such questions can help people to:

- spot issues and frame problems in ambiguous situations
- interpret situations from multiple perspectives
- identify crucial decision points and possibilities for action
- recognize benefits and potential risks inherent in any course of action
- identify and test principles in real classroom situations
- generate new principles that guide instruction

CASES AS A BRIDGE BETWEEN STANDARDS AND CLASSROOM PRACTICE

You may also want to use the standards of the Interstate New Teacher Support and Assessment Consortium (see Table P.1, Intersecting Issues Across INTASC Standards) as a framework for your case analysis. These standards—or a state adaptation of the standards such as the California Standards for the Teaching Profession—are incorporated into many teacher preparation and induction programs around the country. But novices and veteran teachers often have difficulty understanding the relationship between the standards and their work in classrooms.

What is a standard? How might cases bridge the gap between standards and classroom practice? A standard is very much like a *theoretical principle*. It describes how teachers ought to op-

Table P.1. Intersecting Issues Across INTASC Standards

Standards	Cases														
	1	2	3	4	5	6	7	8	9	10	11	12	13	14	15
Content Knowledge/ Pedagogical Content Knowledge	X	X	X	X	X		X	X	X	X	X	X	X	X	X
Social/Emotional/ Intellectual Development	X	X	X	X				X	X	X	X	X	X	X	X
Diverse Learners	X	X	X	X	X	X		X	X	X	X	X	X	X	
Instruction	X	X	X	X	X	X	X	X	X	X	X			X	X
Climate/Learning Community		X	X	X				X				X	X		
Verbal/Nonverbal Communication	X	X	X	X		X		X	X	X	X	X	X	X	X
Planning	X	X	X	X			X	X	X	X				X	X
Assessment	✓	✓	✓	X	✓	✓	✓	✓	✓	✓	✓	✓	X	X	X
Reflective Practitioner	X	X	X	X	X	X	X	X	X	X	X	X	X	X	X
Colleagues/ Community		X	X	X	X	X					X	X	X		

Key: ✓ = Main Idea   X = Relevant Issues

erate in general and, for the most part, without reference to the particulars of person, context, clock, or calendar. The power of a standard is its broad generality, which is also its Achilles heel. A standard is to the policymaker what a theoretical principle is to a scientist.

Teachers are not, by nature, either theoreticians or policymakers. They do not inhabit the universe in general; like most other professional practitioners, they operate in a world of particulars. Teachers function in a world of specific classrooms, particular pupils, and the routines that make the daily life of the school manageable. Teachers tend to design their days and weeks in terms of particular activities, specific subject-matter content, and the trials and tribulations of particular youngsters. Thus, when the individual practitioner, or even a group of teachers, confronts a set of educational standards, he or she encounters a remote abstraction, quite difficult to link to the familiar world of practice.

How, then, are educators committed to a standards-based reform strategy likely to assist teachers in connecting the prosaic elements of classroom and teacherly life to the broad generalizations of standards? Teachers are like many other professional practitioners. Ask a physician about her work and she will more likely tell you the story of her most interesting case than regale you with a theoretical exposition. Inquire similarly of an attorney, and the most challenging case he litigated during the past month will spring to mind. Professionals parse the world of practice using the language of *cases*. Why cases? Because a case is not merely any old story. A case is a singular species of narrative, a story with a point. When the case has a moral or ethical point, we often call it a parable. When it makes a legal point, or a medical point, it can be used by physicians or by lawyers to connect particular events and situations to more general principles, theories, or standards. A story becomes a case when it is a "case of" something and becomes connected to more general principles, policies, or values.

The power of cases for school reform lies in their capacity to create bridges across the great chasm that divides policy from practice. A case is situated between the general power of standards and the rich detail of specific practical situations. By using cases to illustrate standards, or by using standards to illuminate cases, we create a web of meanings and associations between the two worlds. By engaging teachers and other educators in analytic discussions around such cases, in which they create linkages between cases and standards on the one hand, and between cases and their own local work on the other hand, educators become increasingly capable of adapting their work using the "North Star" of standards to guide their pedagogical navigations.

THE IMPACT OF WRITING CASES

In earlier publications, we have examined the case-writing process and the potential impact of that process on teachers' professional lives (see Shulman, 1991; and Shulman with Kepner, 1999). Our data suggest that all the teachers benefited from their collaborative case-writing experience, some more substantively than others. But never has the power of the process been more dramatically evident than with the group of teachers who contributed to this volume. Six months after they had completed their cases, all of the teachers said that the case-writing process had a profound impact on their professional lives. In a video-taped celebratory debriefing session, they reported many examples of instructional changes they had made as a result of their experiences. Examples of these include:

- looking more closely at the relationship between student assignments and assessments
- revising classroom assessments
- influencing change in district assessments
- revising rubrics that were vague and incomplete
- involving students in both their own assessment and the development of new assessments
- dividing instructional methods into smaller parts so students can more readily understand concepts and tasks
- encouraging students to assess one another (e.g., using running records during paired oral reading)
- inaugurating out-of-school remedial classes for students reading below grade level

Why were these teachers motivated to make such changes? What was it about our collaborative writing process and this particular group of teachers that enabled a larger proportion to respond more substantively than others? We have some hypotheses for both questions.

A detailed description of our methods is presented in Chapter 6. Here it is important to note that we use an iterative method that includes several follow-up sessions to provide feedback on case drafts. Editors and case authors work in small groups using both written and oral feedback.

The majority of authors who contributed to this book initiated their case-writing experience with a seminar in December 1998. Unlike previous groups of case writers, many of these teachers had participated in the same teacher preparation and/or support program and had taught in the same district; some even worked in the same school. These similarities may have contributed both to shared ideas about educational goals and to a climate of trust among the teachers as they worked with one another to craft their narratives into compelling cases. Most important, perhaps, all of the teachers were struggling with the challenges of assessment and accountability, which gave the topic of their cases a pressing immediacy. Each of these teachers depicted current challenges and dilemmas in their cases, unlike previous case writers, who often wrote about experiences that happened in the past.

The teachers gave many reasons for the profound impact of the writing experience. Among them were the following:

1. **Time for focused reflection.** Like authors of previous casebooks, these teachers appreciated the time—away from the students—to meet with other teachers and reflect on, deliberate about, and analyze their cases. But unlike some previous experiences when we used the summer for writing, this time we began in December 1998, and were finished by the summer. All the teachers agreed that although they were very busy with the pace of day-to-day teaching, it was important to have an opportunity to step back and reflect *in the midst* of their teaching, so they could immediately try new things and discuss what happened with their colleagues. As one teacher said, "Both the writing and discussion really helped us focus in depth around an issue." Another said: "The whole process was important—writing and discussing. Sometimes it happened in a group, sometimes it happened by myself at the computer, or sometimes just with a partner. Having the in-depth focus is what's important, because we just don't take the time to learn from what we're doing; we just do it!"

2. **Questioning assumptions.** Many teachers looked at their assessment tools in different ways and began to question how and why they were using the assessments. "I really transformed the way I thought about assessment," one teacher said. "I started asking myself, 'What are my students teaching me about the way I'm teaching them?'" They focused more sharply on what they were measuring and why. One noted, "As I was trying to figure out what my case was about, and what I was doing and how I was assessing, I began to wonder: Is it to inspire the kids? Is it to inform the kids? Is it to motivate the kids? What's the best way to report it?"

3. **Empowerment.** This kind of questioning led to increased understanding and empowerment. Many teachers began to see the usefulness of mandated assessments they had simply taken for granted, revising them to suit their needs. One teacher said, "For me it was like this lightbulb that went on," and she and another case author began to revise their rubrics. Others took their cases to their colleagues and district administrators and became the catalysts for major changes in the assessment procedures. When asked why they felt so empowered, one said: "I think it's understanding ourselves and respecting ourselves as professionals. I know what I'm doing here; I know what my students need; and I'm going to make sure that I use something that I know will work and be helpful to me."

4. **Community of learners.** All of the teachers talked about the importance of working collaboratively with colleagues. Besides gaining insights into their own dilemmas, the teachers noted the importance of getting confirmation that others had similar problems. As one teacher said: "It was useful for me to hear people bringing up the same issues that I'm feeling over a specific topic (assessment) . . . and to be able to critique others and help them revise. It also helped me to see different perspectives, like the viewpoint of a teacher advisor helping new teachers." One of the advisors saw a parallel between her advisee's work with students and her own work with advisees. Other

teachers described the significance of the questions that were posed during feedback sessions. As one said, "It was really helpful to me to have other people asking me questions that I wasn't asking myself . . . those kinds of questions challenged what I believe, you know, got me out of my box."

5. **Link between theory and practice.** The question "What is this a case of?" was instrumental in helping the teachers select the classroom dilemma they wanted to deal with, then craft their narratives into teaching cases. Noticing how similar themes popped up in several cases, they began to see how their individual stories made theoretical statements—their cases were instances of a larger class—and they participated in the development of Table I.1, Intersecting Issues Across Cases (see the Introduction). As one teacher advisor talked about the themes she saw in both the advisor cases and her advisee's classrooms, she said: "I used to deal with survival issues with my teachers one at a time. But this [experience] has helped me get thematic . . . [In helping one new teacher] I keep seeing threads going through her teaching . . . it's had a huge, not just a ripple effect . . . a really big effect in the classroom, not only with the work the students produced but with their behavior as well."

AN INVITATION TO JOIN US

Unlike some previous casebooks, cases in this volume are not accompanied by commentaries. During the field test of each case, we gained new insights by engaging in stimulating discussions with a variety of educators. And indeed, some of the educators wrote their own commentaries for their own professional development. Consequently, we decided to broaden the discourse by inviting you to join us by writing your own reactions and interpretations to each case and entering them on our Institute for Case Development Web site, *www.wested.org/icd*, or sending an email message to *icd@wested.org*. We hope to encourage analysis of cases and of case discussions. Utilizing the Internet, we can exceed the boundaries of any individual analysis and help create a community of learners for all who use the cases.

If you are interested in adapting our case development methods to create your own cases, please examine the methodological note and "Guidelines for Writing Cases" (see Chapter 6 and Appendix A) and feel free to adapt any of the methods. If you have a few moments, let us know what you are doing. Like the teachers who write and use these cases, we can always learn from others' experiences.

Judith H. Shulman

REFERENCES

Carnegie Forum on Education and the Economy. (1986). *A nation prepared: Teachers for the twenty-first century*. New York: Author.

Lundeberg, M. A., Levin, B. B., & Harrington, H. L. (1999). *Who learns what from cases and how? The research base for teaching with cases*. Mahwah, NJ: Lawrence Erlbaum Associates.

Shulman, J. H. (1991). Revealing the mysteries of teacher-written cases: Opening the black box. *Journal of Teacher Education, 42*(4), 250–262.

Shulman, J. H., with Kepner, D. (1999). The editorial imperative: Responding to productive tensions between case writing and individual development. *Teacher Education Quarterly, 26*(1), 91–111.

Acknowledgments

We want to thank all of the teachers who contributed to this casebook—and their families—who took more time than they had originally anticipated to craft their stories into teaching cases. We would also like to recognize Susan Schultz, who wrote the Annotated Bibliography; Ellen Moir, Director of the New Teacher Center, who supported this project from the beginning and wrote the Introduction to Chapter 5; her assistant, Sunga Rose, who managed the logistics of many of our meetings with the case writers; and Tim Cuneo, former director of Joint Venture: Silicon Valley Network, for trusting that this project would benefit the teachers in his network. Finally, we are indebted to WestEd's Jim Johnson, who skillfully edited the volume; and our administrative assistant Rosemary De La Torre, who kept track of the various drafts, proofed final copy, formatted the casebook, and kept us all honest.

Judith H. Shulman
Andrea Whittaker
Michele Lew

Introduction:
Framing the Issues and Dilemmas in Classroom-Based Assessment

Andrea Whittaker

"The aim of assessment is primarily to *educate and improve* student performance, not merely to *audit* it."
—G. *Wiggins, 1998, p. 7*

In the past two decades, we have seen state and district accountability systems swing from traditional reliance on norm-referenced, standardized tests to an emphasis on alternative measures that more accurately gauge student performance (e.g., the California Learning and Assessment System [CLAS]). Underlying the shift to more authentic assessments is the growing realization that standardized tests, covering easily measurable skills in multiple-choice and short-answer formats, don't tell us enough about what students actually know and can do, and therefore are of limited value in guiding a teacher's daily instruction. Proponents of the authentic approach, like Wiggins (1998), argue that assessments asking students to create their own responses can better measure the types of problem-solving, analytical thinking, and inquiry skills that today's rigorous content standards demand of students. Furthermore, commercially available norm-referenced tests do not enable teachers or other stakeholders to see how well students are performing relative to specific content standards; by definition, these tests instead provide data about student achievement compared to other students (Popham, 1999).

Yet public and political demands that schools be held accountable for student achievement, the public's assumed familiarity with norm-referenced tests, and parents' desire to know whether their own children are doing at least as well as other students all serve to perpetuate uses of norm-referenced tests.

To bring these two perspectives together, recent work in many states seeks to create standards-based assessment and accountability systems that utilize both norm-referenced and performance-based or extended written response measures (see the Council of Chief State School Officers' Annual Survey of State Student Assessment Programs, 1997; Shields, David, Humphrey & Young, 1999). Recognizing the value of multiple assessments that serve the needs of public accountability yet also inform teachers' day-to-day practice, local administrators have attempted to implement *both* norm-referenced tests and standards-based, performance-based assessments (Shields et al., 1999). All of our case writers teach in districts that have adopted such an approach.

Despite the best efforts of administrators and other educators, occasionally the multiple measures approach, with an emphasis on accountability as opposed to classroom learning, can conflict with school-based reform efforts focused on student-centered teaching, developmental approaches to instruction, and integrated curriculum models. Teachers working within these instructional paradigms need rich, contextualized information about student progress that they can use to continually improve instruction, a need that can clash with accountability systems—driven by state or district mandates, community interests, and/or external funders—that demand quick results and easy-to-produce, easy-to-interpret data (David & Shields, 1998; Koretz, Stecher, Klein, &

McCaffrey, 1994; McDonnell, 1994). In California[1] and other states, recent mandates from the governor's office and state legislature have prompted implementation of complex, quantitative accountability system indices that set criteria for student performance and result in sanctions against low-performing schools (i.e., reconstitution of programs, administration, and faculty if improvement is not demonstrated) and consequences for students (i.e., retention when standards are not achieved). One of our case writers described this context of summative accountability as "accounting" for student achievement or "bean counting" rather than substantive, purposeful, formative assessment of student performance to guide instructional decision-making within their innovative programs.

A FRAMEWORK FOR CASE WRITING AND DISCUSSION

Within this current climate of assessment and accountability, it is especially important to invite teachers into the conversation and encourage them to reflect on their own assessment tools and how and why they are used. Such reflection helps teachers become more critical and informed consumers of assessments, those that others mandate for accountability purposes, and those that teachers design for their own classroom use. In preparing this casebook, we asked teachers to reflect on and write about their experiences developing and using assessment tools ranging from rubrics and performance tasks to portfolios and narrative report cards. We began with a set of six topics loosely based on the framework for "instructionally sound" assessment systems developed for the California Assessment Collaborative's study of 26 school and district performance-based assessment pilot projects (Jamentz, 1993). These topics included:

1. determining what students should know and be able to do
2. designing and interpreting assessments that are faithful to these outcomes
3. incorporating assessments into instruction
4. using those tools and outcomes as the basis for communicating, reporting, and making grading decisions

5. involving students as responsible parties in self-assessment and the monitoring of their own learning
6. using assessments and their outcomes beyond the classroom context

These interrelated topics became our framework for case writing, discussions, revision, and finally, a way to organize and examine the issues within and across the cases presented in this collection. The remainder of this chapter frames the six topics; their corresponding issues, dilemmas, and questions; and their links to particular cases. Table I.1 provides a handy reference showing how each case is linked to each element topic and the related assessment issues. (See Appendix A for the guidelines presented to case writers and Chapter 6 for a methodological note that describes our processes for supporting case writing.)

1. Determining what students should know and be able to do

Beginning with the landmark piece *Standards, Not Standardization*, Wiggins (1991) and others have promoted an assessment reform movement calling for teachers to envision curriculum, instruction, and assessment as an integrated whole. These reformers stress the importance of engaging teachers in articulating targets for student achievement as the basis for developing curriculum and providing instruction that fully engage students in using their minds well. These targets, in the form of content standards, learner outcomes, or essential questions, become the framework and criteria for designing performance-based assessment tools that promote student learning and capture demonstrated performance through various "authentic" means. No longer would teachers and students be confined to paper-and-pencil tests and quizzes to evaluate student achievement of discrete objectives. They could now use standards to define complex tasks and tools that enabled students to demonstrate all that they know and can do. (See *Understanding by Design*, Wiggins & McTighe, 1998, and other assessment resources in the Annotated Bibliography found toward the end of this volume.)

Table I.1. Intersecting Issues Across Cases

CASES	Grade and Context	ISSUES					
		Determining and Using Standards	Designing Assessments	Using Assessment for Instruction	Grading and Reporting	Self-Assessment	Beyond Classroom/ Accountability Issues
Chapter 1 CASE 1	MS/Math		X		X		
CASE 2	Grade 3/LA	X		X	X		X
CASE 3	Grade 2/LA	X		X			X
Chapter 2 CASE 4	HS/Chem.		X	X		X	X
CASE 5	Grade 1/LA	X	X		X		X
CASE 6	MS/LA	X	X	X			X
CASE 7	Grade 6/SS		X	X		X	
Chapter 3 CASE 8	Grade 1/LA	X		X	X		X
CASE 9	Grade 6/LA			X		X	
CASE 10	Grade 5/LA	X	X	X		X	
Chapter 4 CASE 11	MS/LA	X	X	X	X	X	X
CASE 12	MS	X	X		X	X	
Chapter 5 CASE 13	----		X		X		
CASE 14	----	X		X		X	
CASE 15	----			X			

Key: MS = Middle School   LA = Language Arts   SS = Social Studies

Emerging from the performance-based assessment reform efforts of the last decade, standards are ubiquitous in all levels of education today. Virtually every state in the country has determined standards for student learning (Mabry, 1999). National-level subject area organizations have published their own standards for what students need to know and be able to do related to particular disciplines and what teachers need to know and do to prepare them well (i.e., the National Council of Teachers of Mathematics' *Principles and Standards for School Mathematics* [1991] or the National Research Council's *National Science Education Standards* [1996]). Such content standards for student learning are sorted, categorized, and explicated for learners from the kindergarten year to the postbaccalaureate professional development of teachers. There are performance standards that define "how good is good enough" at various benchmark grade levels or transition points from elementary, to middle school, to high school and beyond. Each of our case writers has experienced developing or using content and performance standards for student learning, and many of them have evaluated their own professional performance using state or national standards for high-quality teaching and development.

On the one hand, an absence of standards poses great difficulties for teachers and their students. Several cases in this collection address the thorny difficulties of examining and summarizing students' successes and challenges when expectations for learning are not articulated to teachers or students. In Case 12, a beginning teacher becomes overwhelmed with writing individual narrative report cards for students when expectations for learning are undefined. Similarly, a new teacher advisor (Case 13) tells how she assists a beginning teacher who has not yet determined what she wants students to know and be able to do, nor linked expectations for student learning with her choices of instructional strategies or means for assessing student understanding.

But just having access to content standards that define what students should know and be able to do is often not enough. Several other cases (Cases 5, 7, 11) focus on the curricular challenges of using content standards (developed by schools, district, state, and/or national organizations) in creating units of instruction and related assessment tasks tailored to the needs of individual students. Teachers considered how they determine the desired outcomes for student learning; their relative priorities and compatibility with local, district, state, or national standards; and how to capture such outcomes with assessment tools.

In addition to defining what students should know and be able to do, standards can also determine expectations for when and at what level of quality a student must demonstrate such knowledge and skill. Several authors struggled with the questions, "At what point do students need to reach the standard?" and "How good is good enough?" In Case 11, an experienced teacher grapples with performance standards and the implications for student learning when assessing student writing with a holistic rubric. She also reflects on how she attempts to make the standards clear to students and their parents.

Finally, in recent years, standards-based reform has been used by districts and policymakers to leverage the implementation of high standards and assessment tools designed for high-stakes accountability rather than necessarily serving classroom teaching and learning (Thompson, 2001). Several cases in this collection examine teachers' concerns with assessment tools used to determine which students have met performance standards and the consequences faced by students and teachers when the standard is not reached (Cases 2, 3, 6, and 8).

2. Designing, using, and interpreting assessments that capture student learning

The recent plethora of standards requiring students to produce higher levels of knowledge, thought, and action has generated a whole new assessment technology. Teachers are developing and using a wider variety of assessment tools specifically designed to capture a wider range of student skills, processes, and performances. Such tools include projects, investigations, and open-ended performance assessments in math and science, rubrics and scoring guides for determining qualities of writing in different genres, portfolios for examining progress over time, diagnostic tools such as running records and reading fluency assessments in literacy, and simulations and projects in the social sciences. All of these assessments require that teachers have a sophisticated understanding of the nature of learning; extensive subject matter expertise; and an understanding of reliability, validity, and measurement, and of student cognitive and social development. While these tools open the door to new understandings of what students actually know and can do, they also pose new questions about fairness, equity, reliability, and feasibility. Is a reading fluency assessment designed for English speakers valid when used in a bilingual setting (Baker & Good, 1994)? What are the features of an effective open-ended science problem or investigation that reliably assesses scientific reasoning (Solano-Flores & Shavelson, 1997)? Can a running record or other diagnostic assessment tools be used to determine whether or not a student is retained? Is a rubric too general or too specific to be feasible for routine classroom use (Popham, 1997)? Are the performance standards in a writing rubric grade-level appropriate? When is a standard set too high?

In order to utilize assessment tools thoughtfully and fairly, teachers require substantive professional development to build their capacity to design and implement assessments, and to interpret the data that result. Shepard (2000) recommends that teachers work collaboratively to design classroom assessments that are matched to standards and are an integrated component of instruction that supports a learning culture for them and their students, one that focuses on student learning rather than narrowly defined achievement. These assessments and the data gleaned from them should be a mechanism for helping teachers to examine, revise, and improve their teaching practice.

In too many classrooms, instructional decisions are rarely data-driven and often focus on "covering curriculum," rather than on meeting student learning goals. In contrast, teachers who participate in state or local assessment development, as Shepard recommends, report that this work improves their understanding of the links between classroom uses of assessment, curriculum design, and instruction aligned with standards (Falk & Ort, 1998; Jamentz, 1993; Levine, 1998; Whittaker & Young, 1999). Across the nation, schools and districts have engaged teachers in developing and using local assessments as a means of promoting teacher capacity and, ultimately, student learning.

Our case writers have experienced various degrees of professional development aimed at building their capacity to design, use, and interpret student assessments. Some have participated in school, district, and state-level assessment development. Some have piloted or implemented assessments designed by others for accountability or instructional purposes. All routinely develop and interpret assessment tools for their daily classroom use. Their cases reveal successes and dilemmas in creating appropriate assessment tools; developing scoring criteria, benchmarks, rubrics, exemplars, and scoring guides; using student work as data and/or evidence of student learning; and

deciding next steps for teaching. The cases presented here reflect our case writers' current capacity and continuing needs for professional development. As such, the sample rubrics, tasks, and tools presented here are representative of those developed and used by real teachers. They are not necessarily intended to represent the state of the art in assessment, but rather, what is currently available and in use.

For example, Cases 5 and 6 describe two instances of how teachers work together to develop a reading assessment program that attempts both to fulfill district accountability needs and to provide teachers with student data to guide instruction. Case 5 focuses on a district's efforts in designing a K–2 reading assessment, and Case 6 describes the work of a middle school faculty. Cases 4 and 7 reveal conflicts between instructional practice and assessment choices as individual teachers attempt to design new tools that capture student learning through group work and project-based assignments. Case 4 describes a high school science teacher's efforts to redesign assessment when students reveal to her that the current tools are misaligned with her evolving pedagogy. In Case 7, a sixth-grade teacher is overwhelmed by the time it takes to develop and use complex assessment tools in her social science unit. Issues in all four cases include standard-setting, rubric and scoring design, conflicting assessment purposes, fairness, and the potential misalignment between assessment and instruction.

3. Incorporating assessments into instruction

Ideally, a standards-based classroom integrates curriculum, instruction, and assessment as a three-legged stool. If one leg is not attended to, the others cannot support whoever is seated. In classrooms, it is the student who is seated and his/her learning that can be unsupported when curriculum, instruction, and assessment are not strongly integrated. Real integration means that assessments are embedded in instruction; matched to the goals, formats, and processes of instruction; and provide ongoing learning experiences for students day-to-day. In *Understanding by Design*, Wiggins and McTighe (1998) provide a helpful framework for building such integration through "backwards design." This framework helps teachers first determine the essential understandings of a unit, course, or discipline, then select instructional materials and resources, and determine teaching strategies and student activities with built-in processes and tasks for gathering evidence and evaluating student progress along the way. Such a framework provides teachers with ongoing or "formative" assessment data and results that enable them to diagnose potential stumbling blocks for student learning and determine next steps for modifying instruction through reteaching, revising strategies, or other instructional interventions.

Throughout their professional development as beginning teachers and support providers in the Santa Cruz New Teacher project, many of our case writers have adopted a philosophical and practical stance on the formative, diagnostic, and supportive role of assessment that is well integrated with curriculum and instruction. Consistent with the social constructivist or sociocultural theorists' perspective of "assess to assist" (Tharp & Gallimore, 1986; Vygotsky, 1978), our case writers suggest that assessments embedded in day-to-day instruction should inform the work of teachers by providing data about student progress, and by revealing students' successes and challenges that direct next steps for teaching. These teachers attempt to use standards and assessment tools toward this end. For example, in Case 10 on teaching and assessing analytical essay writing, the author describes how her cycle of teaching, assessment, and revision supports students as writers and informs her own practice as a teacher of writing and a designer of rubrics for assessing writing. Case 1, which depicts assessment as a tool for guiding reteaching, also raises questions about the purposes of formative assessments and their role in helping students to achieve.

However, implementing assessment tools that serve teaching and learning, particularly when designed by those outside the classroom, poses real challenges for classroom teachers. Several of our cases deal with the dilemma of implementing assessments that take too much time away from instruction. We asked teachers to consider how they deal with these concerns and how they integrate assessment into instruction so that the assessment doesn't conflict with instructional goals or come at the expense of instructional time, once again threatening the balance of the three-legged stool.

In Case 7, a well-meaning teacher who valued alternative forms of assessment is overwhelmed by the complexities of implementing performance-based assessments in a series of integrated curriculum projects. Case 3 describes how the task of administering and interpreting diagnostic assessment tools can swallow up time once dedicated to instruction that helped students learn toward the standards. In contrast, the third-year teacher who authored Case 8 describes the value of using an array of assessments embedded in the context of balanced literacy instruction. She argues that these tools provide her with important information about student progress and next steps for teaching.

Cases written by new teacher advisors and presented in Chapter 5 (Cases 13, 14, and 15) also demonstrate how they use diagnostic assessment tools like observation and conferencing within the "assess to assist" philosophy in their work with beginning teachers. They observe, assess, and provide feedback and assistance just beyond the beginning teachers' current level of practice—thus integrating the curriculum and instruction of mentoring with ongoing assessment practices.

4. Using assessment tools for reporting and grading

Once assessment results have been gathered, teachers and schools have an obligation to use these results beyond their own classroom purposes and reveal student progress to a variety of audiences. Communicating assessment results to students, their parents, and other audiences can be a daunting task to even the most experienced teacher. Brookhart (1999) examines grading and reporting practices and offers suggestions to teachers for linking grading practices with classroom-based assessments and for interpreting and reporting the results of standardized tests. Describing the results of norm-referenced, standardized tests, in meaningful language, is complex and often misunderstood by those outside the psychometric community—what does it really mean when a student's reading score is at the 43rd percentile?

Understanding and summarizing the results of alternative or performance-based tools can be just as complex—what does it mean when a first-grade student reads at "level 14," or a third grader has a reading fluency rate of 60 words per minute, or a sixth grader's writing sample gets a "5" on a six-point rubric? How do these performances get translated into grades or become incorporated into report cards or other school-based reporting tools? What are the implications of these "scores" in relation to performance standards set by state or local policymakers?

We asked our case writers to consider how they use a variety of assessment sources for grading, how they incorporate alternative or performance sources into report cards, how they report student progress to parents and other audiences, and how they balance accountability expectations with day-to-day assessments of student progress. Several cases (2, 3, 5, 6, 7, 10 and 11) that examine writing rubrics and reading fluency assessments and one case of using narrative report cards (Case 12) reveal the complexities of these issues. For example, Case 2 examines the role of a reading fluency assessment in determining the reading grade for a bilingual third grader and, despite other areas of creativity and intellectual strength, the consequences of his below-standard score for admission to the school's program for gifted and talented students. In addition, Case 1 questions the role of effort, teacher assistance, and fairness in the assignment of grades.

5. Involving students in their self-assessment and learning

Linn, Baker, and Dunbar (1991) describe a framework for examining the validity of various assessments. Central here is the "meaningfulness" and credibility of an assessment to the students themselves. Truly valid assessments, they suggest, are those students that see as relevant to their learning and life experience, that help them understand their progress and learning challenges. Similarly, Jamentz (1993) argues that in order for assessment systems to be "instructionally sound," students must build their own capacity to under-

stand and use assessment tools to support their ongoing learning. Such capacity-building engages all students in the process of taking responsibility for their own learning. Related issues include setting clear goals, standards, criteria, and expectations for learning; engaging in ongoing reflective dialogue with teachers and peers about learning; and using standards, exemplars of high-quality work, and assessment data to improve their work (Rothman, 1996). Wiggins (1993) also recommends that assessments should offer specific feedback that enables students to make intelligent adjustments to their performance instead of receiving feedback that simply tells learners whether their answers are right or wrong at the end of the testing period. Further, Marzano, Pickering, and Pollock (2001) invite teachers to assist students in personalizing specific standards and criteria through goal-setting, and offering specific and timely teacher, peer, and self feedback. Approaches like these, engaging students in assessing their own work, develop the metacognitive skills necessary to monitor, assess, and redirect future learning—in effect, helping students to learn how to learn.

Several cases in this volume focus directly on methods for assisting students to self-assess. For example, Cases 10 and 11 address the challenges of teaching students about criteria for written assignments through modeling and use of exemplars and rubrics, along with the difficulties students face when assessing and revising their own work. In Case 10, the teacher uses a rubric as a scaffold that informs changes in student performance by providing a target for how to improve their writing and to guide her next steps when students struggle to understand the meaning of the criteria in their own work. Case 11 describes a student who has followed teacher guidelines in a technical sense but who continues to produce writing that does not reach his own expectations.

Three additional cases (9, 12, and 14) examine student self-assessment, self-regulated learning processes, and student goal-setting. In Case 9, a middle school teacher describes how she promotes student self-assessment of learning—not assessment for grading, accountability, or other purposes, but informal assessment of learning through reflection on what makes a "good reader."

She addresses ways to help students be metacognitive about their reading, determining what works well for them and how to improve their ability to comprehend difficult narrative and expository texts. Similarly, Case 14 depicts how a new teacher advisor assists a beginning teacher in her efforts to support middle school students to use "reciprocal teaching" as a means for self-regulation and self-assistance in understanding social science text. Finally, in Case 12, a beginning teacher reveals students' reactions toward her evaluation of their performance when they are left out of the assessment process, difficulties in teaching students about assessment criteria and goal-setting, and how to include them in the process.

6. Using assessments and their outcomes beyond the classroom

As described in the opening paragraphs of this introduction, educators and stakeholders are intensely interested in the assessment of educational outcomes. These include administrators, parents, board members, policymakers, journalists, and members of the general public. Each and every one of our cases has implications for these audiences. All of our cases address the complexities of talking about assessment to these professional and public constituencies and the consequences of such conversations and debates. In particular, Cases 1, 2, 3, and 8 represent the growing public interest in accountability and the resulting increased demands on teachers to produce and report data on student achievement. These cases remind us that not all children come to school with the same experiences, language, knowledge, skills, or familial support, and that along with high standards there must be some safety nets for children to insure equitable educational opportunities and success. Whether the assessment tools are traditional standardized tests or those designed to be more "authentic" to classroom learning, we invite case readers to consider the consequences of high-stakes assessments. As Mabry (1999) suggests,

> Contemporary critics have condemned tests for bias, distortion of curriculum, misalignment with current learning theory and best practices in pedagogy, misallocation of educational resources, deprofessionalization of teachers, demoralization of students and entrenchment of social and political inequities. To the extent that new assessments fail to escape the force field of old measurement ideas and practices, they are subject to the same charges. High stakes concentrate attention on test scores and lock in these negative consequences. Production of test scores overwhelms education as the mission of the school. (p. 676)

AN OVERVIEW OF CASES BY CHAPTER

The six guidelines described above provided our framework for case writing and an introduction to the issues of assessment in today's classrooms, schools, and educational community at large. These guidelines are reframed slightly within five chapters as a means to organize the cases for this book (Table I.1 displays the sequence of cases presented in the book and the issues each case addresses in relation to our original guidelines). Chapter 1 brings together cases that focus on the tensions between assessment purposes—accountability and student learning. Chapter 2 includes cases on designing, using, and interpreting assessments that capture student learning. Chapter 3 reveals cases where teachers have used assessments to guide instruction. Cases in Chapter 4 focus on the links between new forms of assessment and their role in grading and reporting student progress. Finally, Chapter 5 includes cases written by new teacher advisors about their role in assisting beginning teachers to use assessments of many forms.

NOTE

1. California's Academic Performance Index was implemented in 1998 using standardized test score data (from the Stanford 9 test) as the sole indicator of student achievement. Using percentile scores, schools are ranked on a scale of 200–1000 and compared with other schools of similar demographics to determine a "similar schools" score of 1–10. Schools are also required to set and achieve "targets" to move them toward the state goal of a score of 800. Schools and teachers that meet targets receive monetary rewards. For more information, see the California Department of Education web page at http//www.cde.ca.gov.

REFERENCES

Baker, S., & Good, R. (1994, April). *Curriculum-based measurement reading with bilingual Hispanic students: A validation study with second grade students.* Paper presented at the annual meeting of the Council for Exceptional Children/National Training Program for Gifted Education, Denver, CO. [ERIC Document ED 372 369]

Brookhart, S. M. (1999). Teaching about communicating assessment results and grading. *Educational Measurement, 18*(1), 5–13.

Council of Chief State School Officers. (1997). *Annual survey of state student assessment programs, Vol. I and II.* Washington, DC: Author.

David, J. L., & Shields, P. M. (1998). *Pew Network for Standards-Based Systemic Reform: Year two evaluation report.* Menlo Park, CA: SRI International.

Falk, B., & Ort, S. (1998). Sitting down to score: Teacher learning through assessment. *Phi Delta Kappan, 80*(1), 59–64.

Jamentz, C. (1993). *Charting the course toward instructionally sound assessment: A report of the Alternative Assessment Pilot Project.* San Francisco: Far West Laboratory, California Assessment Collaborative.

Koretz, D., Stecher, B., Klein, S., & McCaffrey, D. (1994). The Vermont portfolio assessment program: Findings and implications. *Educational Measurement: Issues and Practice, 13*(3), 5–16.

Levine, E. J. (1998). *Using performance assessment as a tool for reform in an urban school district.* Unpublished doctoral dissertation, Fordham University, New York.

Linn, R., Baker, E., & Dunbar, S. (1991). Complex, performance-based assessment: Expectations and validation criteria. *Educational Researcher, 20*(8), 15–21.

Mabry, L. (1999). Writing to the rubric: Lingering effects of traditional standardized testing on direct writing assessment. *Phi Delta Kappan, 80*(9), 673–679.

Marzano, R. J., Pickering, D. J., & Pollock, J. E. (2001). *Classroom instruction that works: Research-based strategies for increasing student achievement.* Alexandria, VA: Association for Supervision and Curriculum Development.

McDonnell, L. M. (1994). *Policy makers' views of student assessments.* Santa Monica, CA: RAND.

National Council of Teachers of Mathematics. (1991). *Standards for school mathematics.* Reston, VA: Author.

National Council of Teachers of Mathematics. (2000). *Principles and standards of school mathematics.* Reston, VA: Author

National Research Council. (1996). *National science education standards.* Washington, DC: National Academy Press.

Popham, W. J. (1997). What's wrong—and what's right—with rubrics. *Educational Leadership, 55*(2), 72–75.

Popham, W.J. (1999). Why standardized tests don't measure educational quality. *Educational Leadership, 56*(6), 8–15.

Rothman, R. (1996). Linking standards and instruction: HELPS is on the way. *Educational Leadership, 53*(8), 44–49

Shepard, L. A. (2000). The role of assessment in a learning culture. *Educational Researcher, 29*(7), 4–14.

Shields, P., David, J., Humphrey, D., & Young, V. (1999). *Pew Network for Standards-Based Systemic Reform: Year three evaluation report.* Menlo Park, CA: SRI International.

Solano-Flores, G., & Shavelson, R. J. (1997). Development of performance assessments in science: Conceptual, practical, and logistical issues. *Educational Measurement, 16*(3), 16–25.

Tharp, R., & Gallimore, R. (1986). *Rousing minds to life.* New York: Cambridge Press.

Thompson, S. (2001). The authentic standards movement and its evil twin. *Phi Delta Kappan, 82*(5), 358–362.

Vygotsky, L. (1978). *Mind and society.* New York: Cambridge Press.

Whittaker, A., & Young, V. M. (1999, April 5–9). *Assessment, accountability; Assessment per chance to learn—Aye, there's the rub.* Paper presented at the annual meeting of the American Educational Research Association, Montreal, Canada.

Wiggins, G. P. (1991). Standards, not standardization: Evoking quality student work. *Educational Leadership, 48*(5), 18–25.

Wiggins, G. P. (1993). *Assessing student performance: Exploring the purpose and limits of testing.* San Francisco: Jossey-Bass.

Wiggins, G. P. (1998). *Educative assessment: Designing assessments to inform and improve student performance.* San Francisco: Jossey-Bass.

Wiggins, G. P., & McTighe, J. (1998). *Understanding by design.* Alexandria, VA: Association for Supervision and Curriculum Development.

CHAPTER 1

Tension Between Accountability and Student Learning

As described in the intoduction to this volume, the tension between assessment for accountability and assessment for student learning is at an all-time high. Some teachers struggle under the pressure of high-stakes assessments, finding it easier to "teach to the test" and focus on the basic skills being assessed rather than teaching all children to think and learn at high levels of performance. In this chapter, we have provided three cases that examine how teachers attempt to keep the larger goals of student learning at the forefront of their work despite their accountability-driven contexts. In the first case, a middle school math teacher worries that offering too much assistance to a student during classroom testing settings will disadvantage the student when she has to face standardized tests on her own. In the next two cases, high-stakes use of a reading fluency assessment has teachers questioning what they sacrifice in teaching and student learning so that students will reach what they feel is a difficult benchmark.

The remainder of this chapter introduction provides some helpful background reading for these cases and others that follow in later chapters. It provides a research-based overview of reading fluency assessments (used in Cases 2, 3, 6, and 9); and short explanations for running record reading assessments (used in Cases 3 and 8) and two-way bilingual immersion programs (the context for Cases 2 and 3).

UNDERSTANDING READING FLUENCY

Reading research over the past few decades has found a solid correlation between reading flu-ency, or the number of words accurately read in one minute, and comprehension (Allen, 1988; Rasinski, 1990), suggesting that the faster a reader can read, the more s/he will understand. This correlation occurs because if one is reading slowly and presumably struggling to sound out and process individual words and ideas, much of one's cognitive capacity is taken up with this effort and little remains for making meaning of the whole text (Samuels, 1994). Conversely, if sounding out and connecting words into phrases and chunks of text happens with ease, then a reader has more mental energy for piecing together the big ideas, using prior knowledge of text content and structure to make sense of the whole—resulting in good comprehension. Because this correlation can be substantial (as high as 0.80, according to Marston, 1989), those who develop reading assessments have used reading fluency as a proxy for reading performance.

The 1994 National Assessment of Educational Progress (NAEP) study of the oral reading of fourth graders (Pinnell, Pikulski, Wixson, Campbell, Gough, & Beatty, 1995) examined reading fluency as an intricate integration of reading rate (words read per minute), accuracy (percentage of words read correctly), and phrasing (the ability to parse and read chunks of text articulately and with expresssion). In this study, students silently read a grade-level-appropriate narrative text, answered comprehension questions about the text, and then were asked to read the text aloud. They were not told to read the text as quickly as possible, but rather, "to read the story as if they were reading to someone who had never heard it before" (p. 34). Students' performances were rated for accuracy (the percentage of words read correctly), rate (number of words read per minute), and phrasing (size of word groups read, preservation of syntax, and expressiveness). These ratings were compared with each other and the students' overall comprehension score on the NAEP scale (1 to 500). About two-thirds of the students read the text at a rate of 124 words per minute or *slower*, and the one-third of the students with the highest reading rate (130 words per minute or higher) had the highest reading comprehension scores. Additional results revealed that while students with the highest scores on these fluency measures also tended to have the highest comprehension scores, there were some variations. For example, the "relationship between reading accuracy and reading comprehension appeared to be dependent on the nature of students' deviations from the text" (p. 3). Some errors (such as deletions, omissions, and word substitutions) that did not change the meaning of the text did not interfere with students' understanding. As noted in the NAEP report, "even the most fluent readers—make errors as they read" (p. 16). The authors concluded that "although accuracy may play some role in supporting oral reading fluency, there does not seem to be a one-to-one correspondence" (p. 46).

Ideally, such fluency assessments can serve a diagnostic purpose when coupled with other assessments of student reading processes such as running records (as described below) and be used to identify systematic reading errors around which teachers can design instruction. However, as depicted in several cases in this volume, reading fluency assessments are often used singly as a "quick-and-dirty" measure of reading achievement without substantial links to additional assessments that provide a multifaceted understanding of the reading skills and processes necessary for effective reading and understanding, and for planning individualized instruction to support struggling readers.

In the cases in this volume (Cases 2, 3, 6, and 9), teachers have used only reading rate as an assessment of fluency. In contrast to the integrated NAEP process, in these classrooms the reading rate is taken as a student reads an unfamiliar passage orally, often with pressure to read as fast as possible. Only words read accurately are included

in the rating. For example, if a student reads 127 words but makes six errors (which may include the types that do not interfere with comprehension), the score is reduced to 121 words. As described in the cases, students familiar with this assessment quickly learn that speed is the most important aspect of the test. When faced with a comprehension test (most often in the form of story retelling) following the fluency assessment, students often cannot recall much of what has been read. In some instances, the reading rate assessment reinforces the notion that reading is a mindless process to be done as quickly as possible (to get to the bottom of the page) rather than a thoughtful, strategic, and active means for building understanding and appreciation of language, literacy, and literature. This potential outcome is in conflict with the reading instruction goals of many of the authors of these cases.

RUNNING RECORDS AS DIAGNOSTIC READING ASSESSMENT

Originally developed for use in "whole language" classrooms by Marie Clay (1993), running records have become increasingly popular as a diagnostic assessment tool with emergent and beginning readers in "balanced" approaches to literacy instruction. A running record is designed to assess the accuracy of students' reading aloud and the strategies they use while reading. While a student reads aloud an unfamiliar text selected at or near the student's reading level, the teacher records which words were read correctly and when and how a student makes an error or self-corrects. The record is scored for accuracy, and the types of errors and self-corrections are noted. The teacher can use the record to determine if the student is using phonemic awareness strategies and/or visual, semantic, and syntactical cueing systems to self-correct. With this diagnosis, a teacher can determine the kinds of assistance a child might need and how to plan further instruction.

In the last case in this chapter (Case 3), the teacher has not been spending as much time gathering running record data as she has in the past because she feels under pressure to have students reach the reading fluency benchmark. When she observes her students playing at taking running records with each other, she is reminded of their value and revises her approach to include students in assisting one another with this assessment tool.

TWO-WAY BILINGUAL IMMERSION PROGRAMS

Cases 2 and 3 take place in the same school— a school that is implementing a two-way bilingual immersion program. Such programs began in Canada several decades ago as a means for promoting bilingualism and biliteracy in a French- and English-speaking nation. Over the past ten years or so, two-way bilingual immersion programs have become popular and effective methods for teaching English language learners (primarily Spanish speakers in California) and their English-speaking counterparts. The programs are typically designed with equal proportions of monolingual English-speaking students, monolingual Spanish (or other target language) speakers, and students with some level of proficiency in both languages. In the early primary grades the majority of instruction takes place in Spanish (or the target language), and as students move up the grades, more and more English instruction is added until both languages are equally represented in about fourth or fifth grade. Students learn all academic subjects in the target language, and reading instruction in English does not begin until the second or third grade. Based on the assumption that content learning and literacy in one language (usually one's primary language) provide a foundation for future learning and transfers to the second language, these models have a track record of success. Research on programs using this model has demonstrated that both English- and Spanish-speaking youngsters achieve at high levels in *both* languages by grade four or five, and sometimes earlier. In some schools, students who came in using one language or the other are indistinguishable from each other in their use of two languages to read, write, speak, listen, and solve complex problems (Lindholm,

1999). In addition, these schools tend to have additional features that lead to student success, including low mobility rates, teachers and administrators with a common philosophy and instructional approaches, and parent education programs that promote a high degree of participation in school events. Cases 2 and 3 take place in a school that had been implementing this type of program for about 5 years at the time the cases were written.

REFERENCES

Allen, D. D. (1988, November 30–December 3). *Oral and silent reading rates of fourth grade students: Are all good readers fast readers?* Paper presented at the annual meeting of the National Reading Conference, Tucson, AZ.

Clay, M. (1993). *An observation survey of early literacy achievement.* New York: Heinemann Education.

Lindholm, K. (1999, April 5–9). *Impact of two-way immersion elementary program on high school students' attitudes toward school and self.* Paper presented at the annual meeting of the American Educational Research Association, Montreal, Canada.

Marston, D. (1989). Curriculum-based measurement: What is it and why do it? In M. Shinn (Ed.), *Curriculum-based measurement: Assessing special children* (pp. 18–78). New York: Guilford Press.

Pinnell, G., Pikulski, J., Wixson, K., Campbell, J., Gough, P., & Beatty, A. (1995). *Listening to children read aloud: Data from NAEP's Integrated Reading Performance Record (IRPR) at grade 4.* Princeton, NJ: Educational Testing Service; Center for the Assessment of Educational Progress, National Assessment of Educational Progress.

Rasinski, T. V. (1990, November 28–December 1). *Predicting reading rates that correspond to independent, instructional, and frustration reading levels for third and fifth grade students.* Paper presented at the annual meeting of the National Reading Conference, Miami, FL.

Samuels, S. J. (1994). Toward a theory of automatic information processing in reading, revisited. In R. B. Ruddell, M. R. Ruddell, & H. Singer (Eds.), *Theoretical models and processes of reading* (pp. 816–837). Newark, DE: International Reading Association.

CASE 1

Is "Same" Treatment "Fair" Treatment?

Michelle Phillips

"What am I supposed to do here?" Alicia asked as she pointed to the first problem on the quiz.

My eighth-grade algebra class was four days into an inquiry and groupwork-based unit on graphing algebraic equations. On the first and second day of the unit, students took word problems and learned to write equations describing the relationships given in the problem. Alicia had acted as the facilitator for her group during this activity and my observations led me to believe that she had an excellent understanding of how one can describe relationships, using numbers in combination with variables. Now she had a question about the quiz. I attempted to clarify and paraphrase the instructions as best I could without telling her how to do the actual work.

"Well, you need to find some coordinates which make that equation true and then plot them on the graph . . . like we did yesterday." I stood as she stared at the problem.

"What's a coordinate?" she asked.

Was that a clarifying question, I thought to myself? At this point it seemed clear that she hadn't understood our activity from the day before.

But how could that be, given what I had observed in her group? Maybe she understood the concepts but simply missed hearing the term "coordinate." A few of my teacher friends have a rule that students are not allowed to ask any questions during tests or quizzes. They feel that the distinction between clarifying questions and students simply asking how to do the problems becomes muddled, and that the noise involved is distracting to other students. They also feel that teachers answering questions distracts them from keeping a watchful eye out for those less honorable test-takers, and they enjoy staying stationary for a change. I have deliberated on this issue for years. While I understand their contentions, I am empathetic to the student who simply can't get started because there is one word in the directions or one figure that is unclear to them. So my rule has been that "I am happy to answer clarifying questions only" and I usually have no difficulty responding with "Well, that's the part you are supposed to know . . . I can't help you with that." I haven't had trouble drawing that line . . . until this year.

This was the year I was introduced to Alicia. Alicia was one of two African-American students in an eighth-grade class of nearly 300—the second girl was in the special education program. I was teaching at a moderate-size middle school in a wealthy, well-educated, and competitive community with a high level of parental support and involvement. A large proportion of the parents support the movement toward algebra for all eighth graders, and readily hire additional tutors and purchase computer software with the hope of increasing their child's standardized test scores. For reasons that are still unclear to me, Alicia joined the school in eighth grade, taking public transportation from a neighboring city where she lived in project housing with people who were not her parents. She sported a 49ers jacket, Fila tennis shoes, a Tommy Hilfiger cap, and an attitude.

She clearly was not from these parts and I think that's why I liked her from the moment she walked in my door. Alicia was boisterous and spirited, but was never a behavior problem in our class. I was shocked to hear that she had a history of being a "troublemaker" and on one occasion was suspended for threatening my substitute. I had conferred with her counselor, who said she had heard a rumor that Alicia's mother was in jail and her father had always been an unknown entity. Alicia explained to me that she lived with her grandmother; then on another occasion she said it was actually her aunt.

Whoever it was that she lived with, Alicia showed a remarkable amount of courage to come to this school where she clearly did not fit in and was reminded of this fact frequently—by students, teachers, and administrators alike. I was most impressed by her motivation. Her grades were important to her, and her learning was even more important. She readily admitted that she "didn't do good in math" and her standardized test scores were low. We always got along well—I guess we had some kind of unspoken understanding.

"What's a coordinate?" she had asked.

Perhaps while our students learned what coordinates are in seventh grade, Alicia hadn't at her previous school. How would I look at her and say, "Oh, well, you obviously didn't get it—there goes the entire quiz"? Maybe it really was just a matter of defining a vocabulary word—right?

"Coordinates are the x and y values that we were using to find the points on our graphs yesterday—x is the 'input' and y is the 'output,'" I replied reluctantly. A light appeared to go on—maybe it was just the definition.

"So if x is 2, then y would be 5," she said triumphantly.

Ah, relief. She knew how to use the equation, and she got the answer with a minimum of assistance from me. Now I could return to my lookout post. I turned to walk away.

"No, wait . . . don't go," she pleaded.

A couple of students looked up from their quizzes. My assisting Alicia was becoming more conspicuous.

"So I'd put (2,5) over here on the graph," she said earnestly as she incorrectly pointed to the spot where one would actually find (5,2).

Yikes, another large misconception. And students were supposed to have come into the eighth grade with a solid understanding of which line is the x-axis and which line is the y-axis, at least. Well, maybe she understood which axis is which, she just forgot that the x-coordinate comes first in an ordered pair.

That's an easy mistake.

"Well, do you remember which coordinate comes first in an ordered pair?" I asked.

What was I doing?! I was trying to make all possible excuses for her not understanding how to solve the problem—on a quiz! It was obvious that not only did she not "remember," she may not have understood in the first place. And even if it was a simple mistake, it was a mistake nonetheless.

Essentially, I had just told Alicia the answer by not affirming her original conclusion—after all, she had a 50/50 chance. Maybe other students had made this "simple mistake" also, but I wasn't reminding them of the correct answer. Then again, none of them had asked.

But what if they had asked? If Alex, a student who regularly scored 100% on tests and quizzes, had asked, I probably would have responded with something like, "Oh, Alex, you know the answer to that question." He would have smiled wryly, silently agreeing that he probably did know—and if not, he certainly had the strategies to find the solution. If Melilla, a non-native English speaking student, had asked, I probably would have sat with her for a moment, and attempted to help her better understand the instructions. I probably would not have been caught up in these leading questions. But other students didn't ask. Nor did they ever say anything about my helping Alicia.

I shuddered at the realization that not only had more students looked over, but I had spent about five minutes crouched beside Alicia's desk and had essentially led her through an entire problem by giving her three prompts.

I can't remember a time when I answered more than one question per student. And to make matters worse, I still did not have a clear idea of what she really understood. Was I still answering clarifying questions? Hmmm . . . can we clarify what is a clarifying question?

"Oh, that's right," she said matter-of-factly as

she correctly placed a dot after moving two units to the right and five units up.

Had I just "been had," as they say? Was I a sucker? What was it that she really misunderstood? Were her misconceptions the result of simple vocabulary issues, or was there a larger problem? What would this quiz tell me? I had been wary of asking her too many evaluative questions during the quiz itself, because I simply wanted to minimize the disturbance to the class, clear things up for her, and get back to my post. But where should I have drawn the line? I certainly couldn't clarify an entire algebraic concept for her during a quiz. If I were to show her quiz results to her guardian, to a fellow teacher, or to an administrator, they might think that she understood the concept very well. The "A" she received on the quiz might conflict with a standardized or external assessment on the very same concept.

This trend continued to a somewhat lesser degree throughout the year, with students becoming accustomed to Alicia asking more than one question per assessment. Midyear, I asked my students to complete an anonymous survey evaluating the affective components of our classroom and my teaching style.

I recognized her handwriting. Her response to the ambiguous question, "What specific things do I do that help you to learn?" was, "You always answer my questions and help me when I ask." While of course this warmed my heart— having some vague conception of the relatively minimal level of external support she must receive—I couldn't help but feel that in many ways I had done her and the other students a disservice. I worried about the fact that her standardized test scores might not be aligned with her classroom test scores, and that they would not reflect the level to which she acted as a leader in her groups. My ongoing day-to-day assessment of Alicia throughout the year revealed dramatic improvements in her ability in, and attitude toward, math. Her grade in the class reflected this improvement.

But where will she be if she encounters a teacher in the higher levels who has a rule barring questions during tests? I had attempted to stop answering her questions once. I actually said to her, "Alicia, I think that I've been helping you a little too much on tests. I know you can do this on your own, so I want you to try." She couldn't. Repeatedly, she froze on the quizzes when I felt certain that she had understood the material better than most students in the class. "I need your help," she'd say matter-of-factly. Did the effect of my nurturing contribute more to her learning process than an objective test score?

I believe that ultimately, the answer lies in what is the purpose of assessment. If I were using assessment simply to rank the students, Alicia's score would be invalid and I'm certain that other students would have cried "unfair!" (and rightfully so). Surprisingly, they never said that, maybe because they knew that I saw assessment as only one piece of the teaching and learning process. I hoped that if Alicia didn't understand a concept before the quiz, she most likely had a better understanding by the end of the quiz!

When does a teacher become an enabler? If students receive an inordinate amount of help, I worry that they cannot meet the standards on their own.

Given the increased level of interest in and support of external assessments, the teacher's familiarity with the students' reality and ability may play a less significant role in students' future options. It is difficult to find the balance between supporting students in the classroom by differentiating and meeting their very individual needs, and at the same time preparing them for objective evaluation.

Two days before I began my first official, full-time position as a teacher, I was given a piece of advice. The teacher whose vacancy I filled (who had been fired and was subsequently suing the district) stopped by to tell me, "Don't ever let students think you are playing favorites." This tidbit seemed so obvious to me. Of course you don't play favorites as a teacher.

His words have stayed with me through the years, and each time I left Alicia's desk and moved toward the front of the room, they rang again.

At the end of the school year, Alicia said that math was her new favorite subject.

CASE 2

A Trip on the Accountability Highway— Speed Limit: As Fast as You Can Go

Keely C. Floegel

It's toward the end of my second year of teaching and I break no rules, or at least I try not to let anyone find out if I do. No one wants to screw things up in their first few years of teaching. In this profession, rules run the system and the system runs you. Even as a new teacher, that's clear. What is not clear is who exactly makes the rules. The school? The district? The state? It appears that the school is implementing standards mandated by the district that in turn is complying with new state guidelines. Thus, when I began to do my third-quarter grades, I felt that the state of our nation was in my hands. Would I dare pass a child not meeting the standards?

On this new "accountability" highway, teachers are frantically engaging in multiple assessments, gathering and analyzing data, modifying instruction, and reporting results to some mysterious black hole of site administrators, district "result" review teams, and state standard auditors— or whatever you call people in those positions. Then the next quarter comes along and we, the teachers, repeat the cycle all over again: assess, analyze, modify, report; assess, analyze, modify, report. I think about my stamped, filed, and buried scores and humbly ask, Is anyone really looking? Has anyone stopped to think how these assessment demands play out daily in a third-grade classroom? What does this fast-paced highway trip mean to an 8-year-old?

Like all teachers on our staff, I have extremely high standards to follow and take them seriously.

We are one of a handful of bilingual programs surviving California's Proposition 227, which essentially outlawed public school instruction in any language other than English. We gained charter status for our Two-Way Immersion Program, where we provide full literacy instruction in English and Spanish with the ultimate goal that when students graduate from sixth grade at AltaVista School, they are completely bilingual and biliterate. That's no small task, especially with the English-only movement on your tail! Although our school has a unified vision, teachers, administrators, and support staff alike are all faced with the pressure of assessment results and the need to prove on paper the value of what we do. We know it works, we see it daily. But California's anti-bilingual sentiment has put our school under a magnifying glass; our test results for English and Spanish literacy levels are analyzed, as well as anything else non-supporters can find to demolish the possibilities for bilingual programs. So we continually feel the pressure to show evidence that our students are achieving high standards through our program.

This year our school developed new benchmarks across grade levels in various subjects. When our grade-level team began discussing appropriate numbers of words per minute, I took it very seriously. If someone is going to require that a particular level of reading is deemed necessary for improved student achievement on standardized tests and/or for the preparation for more difficult levels of reading, then, by any means necessary, I'll get them there. I never thought, however, that one student and a few words per minute would create such great stress and turmoil that I would want out of the car and off the teaching highway altogether.

THE RACE TO 75 WORDS A MINUTE BEGINS

In my opinion, Alberto was a good reader, just a bit slow. His reading accuracy was 95–100% and his comprehension nearly perfect. Nevertheless, our third-grade level team decided students need to be reading a minimum of 65 words per minute to pass in the second quarter; 75 words per minute was decided as our target for June. From our first conversations, I questioned the importance of words per minute when a student had high accuracy and comprehension. I knew fluency was key, but I wasn't sure *how* important speed needed to be. Part of my resistance stemmed from nervously reviewing the scores from my first assessments. I felt an overwhelming guilt as I committed a cardinal sin in teaching: I actually questioned whether or not some students could realistically reach these standards. Can't all students achieve? I wondered if these high scores would even be possible, and if they were, how was *I* ever going to reach these goals? I also feared we could potentially hinder children like Alberto and his natural love of reading, even if it is still a bit slow.

I was gently reminded by veteran teachers and our collaboration coordinator about the realities of being successful at standardized tests, specifically the SAT 9 in English and the SABE2 in Spanish. I could live with that; it even made sense. "Fine," I started to encourage myself. "We can read faster, and we'll aim to surpass the 75 words per minute goal!" I had total faith in myself and my students. "We can do this!" I became excited at the challenge and off we went. Alberto began, syllable by syllable.

29 words per minute . . .

Low scores, more room to improve! I knew it would be a long road, but I never doubted his

dedication to learning or my dedication to helping him and all my students improve their reading. It became a game in the classroom; Alberto and many others began reading all the time, even in their free time. Various students started a University Club for students who wanted to read at lunch. They read fast, slow, with teacher voices, and with animal voices. They read like Martians, they read like Earthlings.

33 words per minute . . .

Only twice as many words per minute to go! The positive energy was high, and low numbers didn't get us down as we entered our parent-teacher conference in September. I enjoy conferences with all my students' families because together we create long-term, student/teacher/parent goals. Without having to mention reading, Alberto's mother commented, "*¿Mi hijo debe leer un poco mejor, no?*" (*My child should be reading better, right?*) We discussed his strengths in comprehension and accuracy as well as ways to practice speed-reading. The family committed to reading at home every night for at least 10 to 15 minutes. We discussed our goals on how fast he should be reading. We aimed for 45–50 words per minute by December. Was I setting them up for failure? Was this too high to reach by then? Was it not high enough to get him to 75 (at least) by June? We hopped in the car and began our journey. Over the next few months at home, they tried reading aloud, timed reading, reading easy books and magazines, reading letters, and reading the same text simultaneously.

45 words per minute . . .

Now I knew we were getting somewhere. With the family at home, the friends and teacher at school, there was no stopping this fast-moving car. Sixty-five words per minute just up ahead! At school we continued reading games and added a few new strategies. Alberto read with higher readers, trying to keep up. He read with lower readers, pushing them to read faster, too. He timed himself, and we kept a bimonthly record of various texts he was reading as well as samples of third-grade reading benchmark assessments. He went to kindergarten to help with reading, he read big books, and he taped himself reading.

49 words per minute . . .

Aside from his reading, I had noticed Alberto had a high interest and natural ability in science. Daily he left me dumbstruck with thoughtful and invigorating questions about the living world around us. I recommended Alberto for GATE — the Gifted and Talented Education Program — which at our school is focused on science. Students participate at a local Science Center, learning and making science experiments on color, sounds, and electricity (among many other things), then bring an experiment back to the classroom to teach to their peers. It's perfect for Alberto. I believe one of our most important roles as teachers is finding such opportunities for each of our students, whether their interest is music, soccer, animals, dance, or firefighters. I think attending GATE helped Alberto become more enthusiastic about learning, and even more dedicated to reading! I will never forget his glowing eyes as he entered the classroom with a mechanical color wheel they had just created in GATE. As if by magic he elevated the pieces in the air and strategically united a small red wire to a battery end, and the paper wheel colored in organized patterns of red, white, and green began to spin freely. "Look, look what new colors we can make!" The students surrounded him with amazement. So did I. It was magic!

In third grade, students don't have to meet the specific requirements for GATE because it is their first time receiving grades. Teachers have the liberty to *select* students who would possibly fit the GATE program, without following strict criteria. As long as Alberto kept improving on reading, I kept him in GATE.

51 words per minute . . .

It was December and the stopwatch clicked 56, 57, 58 seconds and Alberto's words were going up, 48, 49, 50, 51 words per minute. I could hear faint whispers of the sappy *Chariots of Fire* theme while watching Alberto running down the beach in victory! We made our goal! I was so

proud of our entire class and of his family! Alberto received much recognition for his effort. His family received the "Read-Aloud" award at our December Family Night. In class we celebrated all of the various individual victories and, of course, Alberto was the star. In all the excitement, however, I heard myself playing my own rather depressing broken record repeating the same message over and over: "Good, now faster. Good, now faster." I was exhausted from the pressure, knowing only half the journey was complete. Was he exhausted, too?

After recognizing all the victories, the first semester ended and students were off to vacation and report cards were going home. Alberto received the "Capital N," or "No Passing" grade in Reading, but it was OK, the standards were clear: 65 words per minute to pass. He is a confident child with a supportive family. No one felt bad about the N, including me. It just meant he had a little ways to go. We still had half a year to meet the 75 words per minute goal. As he left for a month-long vacation, I reminded him of his goals: Read, read, read!

Immediately upon returning to school in January, I tested him. I was back on that highway, time was running out: "Get in the car, Alberto!" I frantically shouted as I drove away and Alberto was still shutting his door. Assess him, gather the data, analyze it, and modify my instruction accordingly. It felt as if I was sending him the message, "Never mind how vacation went, let's deal with your speed-reading!" I was so relieved to discover that Alberto came back reading faster than ever! He had dedicated himself to the books, and was ready to reach the big 75 words per minute goal.

59 words per minute . . .

Part of me wondered if the text was too easy. Should I retest? Did he really read 59 words per minute? Who after a month of vacation comes back sharper than when they left? I retested.

59 words per minute . . .

A solid 59—that's a good sign, now let's keep moving him forward. Then I overheard a conversation regarding GATE for the next school year:

all As and Bs, *absolutely no Ns.* As the GATE director continued to rattle off a bunch more information on standardized test scores, I interrupted: "What?" I knew that GATE was limited to exceptionally gifted students for a reason. He clarified that the second-semester grades were going to be analyzed for GATE criteria the next year. With Alberto's reading still at 59 words per minute, I began to question: Would I pass him? Could I? Is he still a GATE candidate?

59 words per minute . . .

Still 59 words per minute, and I was panicking. I wanted off the highway and onto a nice country road. "N-Day" had arrived too soon. Would this go down in history as the day Alberto once again received a "No Pass" grade for hard work and phenomenal progress in reading? Our time was up; third-quarter grades were going home the next day. I don't know if this is cheating, but we read the exact same text again. I was desperate for more words! I was stressed! I wanted him to pass! Let's put the car into sixth gear! Faster, Alberto, faster!

61 words per minute . . .

Higher, but 61 words per minute still didn't make the grade. The car came to a screeching halt. The "No Pass" reading grade was about to embark on its slow and painful journey to Alberto Garcia's home. All year I had acknowledged the hard work of both Alberto and his family. The progress we made together at home and in the classroom was extraordinary. We more than doubled his speed in less than six months. Everyone put in 110% effort. What more could we ask for? I knew the answer to that question: at least 65 words per minute. Third-quarter report cards became the battleground for my own personal tug-of-war. The only injured party would be Alberto Garcia. Back and forth I struggled, my brain battling my heart: high standards versus the classroom realities of student progress, teacher judgment, and effects grades have on acceptance into special programs like GATE.

That same day we had a third-grade collaboration meeting. I asked my colleagues, "What would *you* do? We've got high comprehension, high accuracy, and 61 words per minute." After asking, it seemed like a dumb and unnecessary question. "Of course you pass him," immediately responded the collaboration coordinator. "No doubt," said another. Everyone agreed and started to continue with the agenda. Of course, I was happy hearing what I wanted to hear, but inside I felt unsatisfied. I kept questioning, unable to answer. What is the purpose of having the standard if we were ultimately not held accountable for meeting it?

At that same moment, in the middle of the turmoil of grading, the school site decided to raise our required words per minute from 75 to 95 for next year! Of course, the stress level led me into a defensive battle with the numbers. Why? What would happen to Alberto in this situation? Would his scientific genius ever be discovered with standards in reading that were quite possibly unattainable for him at this time? "Focus," my team reminded me, these numbers were for next year. I was outraged at the new top-down decision and concerned about next year's students. For the moment, however, I needed to focus on Alberto and his reading grade.

It was time to talk to Mom and Alberto together. They knew he didn't have the numbers to pass, but the combination of his progress, comprehension and accuracy was definitely a solid B. Not only did I pass him; I gave him a B! They'd need to keep working on reading, but I once again acknowledged their efforts and encouraged them to keep up the good work

After third-quarter grades went home, I was left with an uneasy satisfaction and squirmed with anxiety. Would his words per minute naturally have gone up? Would his mother's instincts and mine have naturally led him to the same place without the circus of numbers? Is this just a case of new teachers needing to learn the system and decipher between which standards *matter* and which don't? If so, this is not the way to indoctrinate new teachers into the system. I decided it was time to do something different: I decided to take a big risk and quit worrying about it. Maybe not meeting the standards would force the being from the mysterious black hole of assessment results to show his face. I don't really know why I would want to see the man within the black hole, nor do I know what I would say to him. What I do know is that the bureaucracy of assessment results has us teachers so overwhelmingly busy that we don't have time to ask the simple questions of *who* is in charge of our data, *why* certain data are required, *what* the data are used for, and most importantly, *what* is the research basis for particular standards-based decisions.

I am currently doubting my teaching, questioning my strategies. I wish I felt completely at ease with the fact that I passed a child in reading below the school grade level expectations, but I don't. Part of me is proud knowing that for next year at least, the number of words per minute will not restrict Alberto from the opportunity to participate in GATE. Yet part of me wonders if I've let the whole system down—the state, district, the school (Alberto and myself included)—by not holding him to those same high standards. What exactly does it mean to hold high standards?

I wish I could say that this is one student in one classroom in one district. However, that is not the case. There were many solid readers in my class and throughout our grade level with high accuracy and comprehension who didn't cut the words per minute. In my class of 20, there were three in Alberto's same position. Each of five third-grade classes had their handful of similar

cases. I made one, *and only one*, exception. I ask myself, have the standards held us accountable for our teaching and student learning? Or have they created an unnecessary and overwhelming tension between what we assess in our students, how we move them forward in their learning, and, most importantly, what we teach?

I also wonder how meeting the benchmarks affected my instruction. Obsessed with the notion of meeting the needs of all 20 students in my classroom, I struggled to keep them continually moving forward. Conferences with every family at the beginning of the year focused on setting goals for reading, and every family and child worked to reach those goals. But if a child reached a benchmark, then it became a game of on to the next goal: If they met the third-grade benchmark, try the fourth-grade one, and so on. When is enough, simply enough? How much am I sacrificing my goal of getting students to enjoy reading and learning by constantly pushing them to reach a higher benchmark?

I obviously don't have the answers, but I know one thing for sure. Assessment gives us the information we need to help steer us forward. At what point are we, the teachers and students, allowed to drive the car? When will we be allowed to choose the desired speed, make stops as necessary, and veer toward interesting sights? After all, we are the ones making the journey.

CASE 3

Does the End Justify the Means?

Kathleen Flowers

"Stop! You're reading too fast!" I barked, flabbergasted by a 7-year-old who was reading so quickly I could barely comprehend her, let alone make the obligatory tick marks meant for each word of the reading assessment tool I was using. Carolina shot a look that pierced me to the core. She sized me up, let out a *"puft"* sound, rolled her eyes and looked away. I swear I heard her thoughts: "Get it straight, Teacher. I thought you wanted us to read as fast as we can."

She had every right to be disgusted with the ironic situation I had created. For two weeks I had been focusing all my attention and time on helping the less fluent readers in our second-grade class improve their words per minute count. But when it was finally one of the class's highest reader's turn to perform, I snapped at her to stop in the middle of her shining demonstration to reprimand her for doing too well. What kind of mixed-up message was I giving? How could I have gotten so obsessed with the conquest of one isolated skill? With regret, I realized that I had been fostering an adversely competitive atmosphere in which students were given the message that they could only receive the teacher's attention if their skill level was low. As a result, I had not only alienated students from one another, but worse, estranged them from the very reasons I wanted them to become fluent readers in the first place.

This is my third year of teaching. I teach second grade at a public school in a farming community in California. Of the 12 girls and 8 boys in my class, 95% are Latino, the other 5% African American. Spanish is the primary home language of 75% of my students. Most of these children are first- or second-generation immigrants from Mexico. Nearly half qualify for migrant services; three-quarters receive free or reduced-price school breakfast and lunch.

Our school is midway through constructing a Two-Way Bilingual Immersion Program. We began five years ago with kindergarten, each year adding another grade until the program runs schoolwide from kindergarten through the sixth grade. At present, our Two-Way Bilingual Immersion classes are entering the fifth grade. The goal of this program is to produce English/ Spanish bilingual, biliterate, and multiculturally aware students who excel academically and socially by the time they graduate from the sixth grade.

Contrary to public opinion in California, an abundance of evidence proves the success of bilingual education, with exceptional results yielded from this two-way model in particular. The parents of our students wholeheartedly support the motivations, methods for, and results generated by what we are doing in our classrooms. Despite this overwhelming endorsement, Proposition 227 dealt bilingual education a dreadful blow, making it essentially unlawful to speak any language other than English in the classroom. The best antidote our school could find for continuing our instruction in both English and Spanish was to become a charter public school. We were not alone in choosing this alternative. Four other two-way bilingual immersion public schools in the state

Using Assessments to Teach for Understanding: A Casebook for Educators. Copyright © 2002 by Teachers College, Columbia University. All rights reserved. ISBN 0-8077-4214-7 (pbk.). Prior to photocopying items for classroom use, please contact the Copyright Clearance Center, Customer Service, 222 Rosewood Dr., Danvers, MA 01923, USA, tel. (508) 750 8400.

were also recognized for the success of their programs and granted charter status to avoid the new law.

While I am in favor of program accountability, I disagree with the way that assessment ends up focused on merely the results from standardized tests mandated by the state. Clearly, the state may need to come to agreement about some kind of uniform performance measurement among the different schools. However, to entirely dismiss the diverse and authentic forms of assessment that teachers use to gauge what is actually learned in the classroom in exchange for the single set of scores that standardized testing conveniently provides is an inadequate and shortsighted solution.

At the school where I work there is a lot at stake for our students to do well on these standardized tests. Their scores may be one of very few factors taken into consideration in the debate on whether or not we retain our public school charter status. And of course, without charter status we would have to abandon the bilingual program that our students' parents desire and support. But by focusing so much energy on the outcomes of standardized testing, I end up sacrificing the multiplicity and complexity of ways through which I as a teacher actually learn about what my students know and what I still need to teach them. I find myself spending an absurd amount of time preparing my 7-year-old students with strategies for just understanding how to cope with a fill-in-the-bubble standardized test when there is so much, much more they need to learn in not only one, but two languages!

Back to my story. In my first two years of teaching, I felt that I was using every ounce of my concentration, effort, and training to get up to speed in the profession. I worked 60-hour or more weeks strengthening my knowledge of the content matter, familiarizing myself with the school and district standards, creating integrated thematic units, and figuring out numerous kinds of assessment procedures. Even as frazzled and fatigued as all of this scrambling around made me, I still had the sense that our classroom was a vital and exciting place where all kinds of learning was going on. The students did well and showed signs of feeling genuinely empowered to share their opinions and to take intellectual risks. I was inspired to

show up every day just to see what we would explore and teach each other.

But something changed this year. It began to creep up on me, this awareness that I was losing sight of the reason I came into teaching. I had wanted to share my love of learning with children. In return, their enthusiasm and curiosity to dive into ideas with pure 7-year-old passion and excitement inspired me. At the beginning of this year, we delighted in the rich discussions inspired by the books we read aloud. We spent afternoons devoted to finding just the right adjectives to complete our shared class poem. These activities sparked great debates on things like synonyms and author's style. However, by the second quarter, literacy and higher thinking–type strategies were being replaced with a tangle of tedious and time-consuming assessments. In the first week of February, it dawned on me that I hadn't led one small literature discussion group since before leaving for winter break in mid-December! Instead, I was consumed with the assembling and recording of little numbers that I would add to the school's database next to each student's name: the score for their reading level, the percentage of correctly answered comprehension questions, and even more hair-splitting, the number of words they could read per minute.

My grade-level team had decided that the best way to gather and evaluate the data regarding the reading progress of our students was to give them individual tests for reading level, comprehension, and words read per minute each quarter and keep track of their progress. We set benchmark levels for where they were supposed to be in each of these three areas in Spanish literacy. What we observed was that the classes naturally organized themselves into three distinctive groups. One group could be classified as at or above grade level, the next hovered just below grade level, and then there was a group that was basically a grade level behind. The students who qualified for formal[1] English Reading instruction met a certain criterion (no matter what their first language happened to be): they needed to be at or above grade level in both Spanish reading and in English language fluency.

The rationale behind this criterion was that studies have conclusively shown that once children learn to read fluently in one language, they can apply this skill to another language in which they have adequate comprehension and familiarity. Happily, I have observed that this transition happens quite rapidly and effectively as long as the literacy skills in the first language are solid and the process is not rushed. By the end of second grade, 60% of my second graders met this criterion and were receiving formal English reading instruction.[2]

In my particular second grade class of 20 students, the speed-reading Carolina was one of the 14 children at or above grade level. Two fell just below grade level, and four were reading at first-grade level in the primary language of instruction, Spanish. Once my colleagues and I saw how the reading abilities were organized, we decided to target those students in the middle who appeared to need a little push. We figured that since time was of the essence, we could count on the ones at grade level or above to keep progressing via reading on their own and in whole-class activities. And since the ones at the bottom were already receiving 45 minutes of special literacy tutoring every day from our trained reading aides, it was the middle group that would benefit most from our focused attention.

After asking around, a colleague shared with me that she had had lots of success by explicitly communicating with students where they presently measured on the reading rubric and indicating where they needed to go to be at grade level. She strived to do this in such a way as not to demean or demoralize the children. It was her aim to acknowledge their potential while asking for their participation in setting personal reading goals. So that is what I tried with my two students who read just below grade level. While Sam and Geraldo each appeared unconcerned by learning their individual reading scores, they both listened respectfully during our little talks about the progress they needed to make. However, when it was time for them to contribute, they didn't seem overly motivated by the whole endeavor. And why should they be? They had been perfectly content spending our daily quiet reading time either flipping through picture books at the speed of light or distracting others from their books. It didn't take a genius to realize that reading was not on

the top of their "Favorite Pastimes List." What could I do to inspire them?

Like all good blunders, I hatched my plan innocently enough and with the best of intentions. I designed these nifty certificates on the computer and decorated them with cool stickers. Each time any student in the class jumped to a higher reading level or increased the amount of words read per minute, they received one. I took it as a positive sign that the students treasured and collected these certificates like gold and proudly shuttled each one home for parental inspection and adulation. But Sam and Geraldo didn't progress fast enough. So I didn't stop there. One afternoon, in a moment of desperation for quicker results, I fell back on the kind of reward systems my mother employed (and I enjoyed) when I was a child: food. I made the impulsive offer of a McDonald's lunch to any student who could meet their required reading levels!

I wish now that I could have foreseen the commotion this seemingly innocuous offer ignited. While Sam and Geraldo dedicated themselves entirely to the pursuit of this culinary trophy, two thirds of my students (those who had already met or surpassed the grade level reading benchmarks) made strong cases for the injustice they suffered by being excluded from the contest. They were right. I was, in essence, telling them, "If you are doing well, then good for you. Don't rock the boat. The teacher doesn't have any time or interest in your reading. But if you're struggling a bit, well, we'll drop everything and barrage you with a battery of tests and prizes."

The debate led to an impromptu class meeting in which I tried to rationalize the obvious inequality of treatment by talking about how all of us excel in certain areas, while others require a little additional effort. I explained that those students who had the chance to go to McDonald's would have more than earned it by lots and lots of extra work and determination. I described in detail how these exhausted students would be giving up part or all of their playtime to do even more work with their families in the pursuit of reading faster and better. When this explanation did not placate the majority, I finally settled the dispute by offering a pizza party for the whole class at the end of the year. We would celebrate how much progress everyone had made in their reading ability.

I was treading on slippery ground, and I knew it. As I looked out upon the class circle, I noted the angry, disappointed, and uncomfortable faces looking back at me. I recognized that I was feeling pretty awful myself. How had we gotten so far away from what reading is all about to begin with? Didn't I want to teach kids how to read because it can bring so much enjoyment and enrichment? Had I become so caught up in proving to the bilingual education skeptics, the policymakers, the voters, and the grant providers that our program really could work if given half the chance, that I forgot who I was there to serve and for what purpose?

While I was spinning in my own quagmire of these educational and ethical questions, Sam and Geraldo, on their own initiative, buddied up and engaged in a friendly competition to meet their reading goals. After lots of practice, improvement, testing, and more practice they earned their McDonald's lunches on the very same day! We had a great celebratory time and I'm happy to report that reading is not the only accomplishment that was achieved in the circuitous process I bungled through. On top of reaching grade level in their reading abilities, they've also gone from occasional participants in class to regularly offering their input. The really encouraging thing is that Geraldo has become a lover of reading who steals away every chance he gets to work his way through longer books he keeps stashed in his desk. Whereas before he would groan when I would invite him to read to me or aloud in a small group, now there's not a day that goes by when he doesn't beg me to listen to a story he's engaged in. Although Sam's interest in reading has not made such a radical turn, I am happy to report that he is using the class silent reading time for something other than speed-illustration gazing. At the moment, he has discovered a series of science books that describe in detail amazing facts about different animals. He was even spontaneously inspired to get one during a whole-class discussion so that he could show us something he had learned about amphibians while reading the day before.

Through their actions, these two students conveyed to me that competition, when structured in a thoughtful way, does not need to be thrown out altogether. Instead of focusing on doing better than the other person or becoming fixated on the prize, these two boys helped one another actually become better readers. In doing so, they discovered that reading was something they liked to do after all.

On another day, Carolina and another little girl taught me another lesson in how to change the dynamic and focus around this whole reading assessment dilemma. Just as I was about to separate them for playing during silent reading time, I hesitated just long enough to observe what they were doing. One was reading her book aloud while our rapid reading Carolina was making little check marks for every word the other read. They were playing Teacher and giving each other Running Record Assessments![3] Of course! Once again it was the children who held the key to unlocking the most stubborn of predicaments! Why hadn't I thought of it?

I knew that in second language acquisition one of the crucial components of an effective program is surrounding students with as many native speaker models as possible. It just makes sense that the more teachers you have in an environment, the more opportunity for learning. In every classroom there is an unlimited source of intelligence, creativity, and enthusiasm that can be harnessed so students are teaching one another the very things they themselves are excited about grasping. Better yet, they teach in ways that make sense to one another. Why not designate Buddy Reading Times on alternating days instead of always having students read to themselves or with me in a small group? By doing this, their fluency would have lots more opportunity to develop and improve. By explicitly teaching the students how to and for what purpose one gives the Running Record Assessments, I would be giving them the whole reading picture instead of isolating the separate skills.

This new experiment would also address some of the challenges I face as I try to meet the diverse learning needs, styles, and levels of all of my students. Tutoring one another would force the more fluent readers to metacognate about what they were doing so that they could figure out how to more effectively teach their buddies. By sharing their own strategies and explanations about reading, they would reinforce these successful habits for themselves. At the same time, the "at-risk" students would get a chance to shadow the proficient readers so that they could see what they were working toward while receiving valuable help and encouragement. Besides, you can bet that it sounds more appealing to a 7-year-old to work with a buddy than always getting singled out for remedial help and testing from the teacher. Other benefits of this new strategy would be that in addition to having more teachers per capita, students would take more responsibility for their own learning. Students would work cooperatively, instead of competitively, toward achieving goals they set for themselves. The teacher would be free once again to concentrate her energies on using diverse and comprehensive strategies with students toward the aim of reading and enjoying literature as critical and creative thinkers.

I see now that in my desperate attempt to push a few students toward achieving grade level reading fluency, I had lost sight of the essential reasons why I want my students to become fluent readers in the first place: to make connections to the text with their own life experiences or with prior knowledge; to read efficiently enough to think critically and creatively about the text; and most importantly, to be engaged in and enjoy the process of reading.

I am left chewing on so many questions and concerns caused by this assessment debate. I know that students need to read well and efficiently in order to want to be readers and that teachers need means for evaluating these skills. However, by giving too much weight to the grade-level benchmarks set by my school and the district, I ended up casting away activities that promote the overall essential skills and attitudes that I want my students to walk away with at the end of the year. These include a lifelong passion for learning, the practical know-how for being responsible and caring members of the community, and the awareness that their life experience and knowledge are valuable resources that need to be shared. I do not believe that as the teacher I am the exclusive proprietor and downloader of infor-

mation and wisdom that fills the empty vessels of my students' minds. Instead, I grapple with how I can encourage a spirit of camaraderie among my students and myself that channels all of our extraordinary energy and enthusiasm as a room full of teachers and learners. I worry that if, for erroneous or superficial motivations, I inadvertently crush curiosity, self-esteem, and esprit de corps so early in their lives, what kind of future for the world am I cultivating?

Maybe it's naive of me, but I wish that communities would put more emphasis on promoting the training, experience, intuition, and sense of appropriate instruction that teachers bring to their classrooms. The public might invest their well-meaning concern better by asking teachers themselves how they teach and assess, and why. I would bet that by engaging in this kind of conversation, the public might come away with a bit more understanding and even confidence in the ability of teachers to assess how students are doing and in assisting them in the areas in which they need to progress.

As specifically regards literacy instruction, I wonder what kinds of truly authentic reading assessment practices could be tailored to the diverse needs of the different students in my class. How could I meet certain desired outcomes and standards without giving up too much critical instruction time? How could I simultaneously challenge the skillful readers and assist the ones who are almost proficient, while not relegating the slower readers to the sole instruction of teacher aides who are not credentialed? Besides, where does the reality that children develop their reading skills at their own different developmental rates and ages factor in? Will there ever come a day when policymakers take a hard look at the occasional adverse effects of pushing all of the students to attain the same level of proficiency at the same time?

NOTES

1. I use the term "formal English reading instruction" to denote those children who are ready to work in small groups reading books at their level of English

reading development with the instruction of the teacher. Otherwise, since the first day of Kindergarten, all students are exposed to English print in many ways: students follow along as teachers read aloud from Big Books, recite poems, sing songs from charts, etc.

2. Traditionally, in Two-Way Bilingual Immersion programs, reading instruction in the second language does not happen until at least the third grade. However, again because of external pressures from the district and state, we find ourselves pushing to accelerate this process with the hope that we are not jeopardizing the final outcome.

3. A form of reading assessment created by Marie Clay.

CHAPTER 2

Designing, Using, and Interpreting Assessments That Capture Student Learning

Recognition of the value of multiple measures of student achievement has created new responsibilities for teachers. In addition to implementing state-mandated standardized tests, many teachers are designing, using, and interpreting new performance-based assessments. The teacher-authors in this casebook have had a range of professional development experiences aimed at building their capacity to develop, implement, and analyze assessments. Some have just begun participating in assessment-related professional development activities at a school and district level, while others have been engaged in statewide professional development programs in assessment for years. The cases presented here reflect various teachers' successes and dilemmas in shaping and introducing new assessment processes.

Cases 4 and 6 describe two instances of teachers' frustration with particular assessments and their subsequent awareness of the need to design different, more meaningful kinds of evaluations. In Case 5, two teachers document their school district's efforts to develop a reading assessment program that both fulfills district accountability needs and provides teachers with data to guide instruction. The teacher in Case 7 values multiple forms of assessment but struggles with the complexities of implementing a host of performance-based assessments in an interdisciplinary unit. Collectively, the cases in this chapter examine issues of standard-setting, rubric design and scoring, conflicting assessment purposes, potential misalignment between assessment and instruction, and fairness. The cases also highlight how time-consuming it can be for teachers to effectively create and implement assessments that capture student learning.

CASE 4

Exploring Alternative Assessment

Susan E. Schultz

It's hard to believe a ten-letter word can cause such anguish to educators in general and account for numerous hours of torment for me.[1] *Evaluation* of groupwork activities raises some really tough questions, with many unresolved answers.

I teach chemistry at a public high school that has some of the richest and the poorest students in the San Francisco Bay Area. Approximately 50 ethnic groups are represented by our students, and my chemistry classes are an excellent reflection of the school's ethnic and academic diversity.

During my seven years as a teacher, I have tried a number of teaching techniques. In the last two years, I added Complex Instruction[2] as a major tool in my teaching repertoire. During the first month of school, I taught a unit on the concept of density—typically a difficult idea for students to understand. I created the four-day unit, called The Ups and Downs of Things, using the curriculum design principles of Complex Instruction. My goal was to provide an opportunity for students to discover that all substances have a specific density and that density is the ratio of mass to volume for any substance. On the first day, each group performed a different activity that concentrated on the central question "What is density?" Only I knew the question, however. I had intentionally avoided using the word "density" when I'd introduced the activities. I wanted my students to perform various activities and then hypothesize the central question or idea.

One group had a large bucket and 20 different items. The members hypothesized and stated their rationale for which objects would float and which would sink. Then the group designed and conducted an experiment to test its hypothesis. Finally, the students created a table to illustrate their results.

The second group experimented with four unknown solutions that contained different food coloring. Using a potato and a drinking straw, the members determined how the four liquids could be separated into distinctly different layers. The group tested the liquids and completed a visual display for the class.

A third group read a story about two women hiking in the woods. The women stumble upon a small stream and decide to leave their Coke and Diet Coke cans in the water to keep them cool. When they return, one of the cans is missing. The group had to hypothesize which can was missing and then justify the hypothesis. I provided a large bucket of water and cans of Coke and Diet Coke to assist the group in its exploration. Finally, the group wrote a letter to the two women explaining what had happened.

Another group measured the mass and volume of a number of metal samples. The students used a scale to weigh the samples and used a water displacement method to calculate the volume. After collecting the data, the members plotted the information on a graph and analyzed the relationship between mass and volume.

At the end of the period, students all completed an individual report (see Figure 4.1, individual reports of activities 1–4) responding to a few

FIGURE 4.1. Individual Student Reports, Activities 1–4

THE UPS AND DOWNS OF THINGS !!
Key Idea: In what ways do ups & downs of things affect our lives?

Activity #1 What sinks and why?

Individual Report #1

Life jackets are an integral part of boating in the U.S. Even when you rent a paddle boat, you are required to use a life jacket, and when a boat or ship capsizes or a plane goes down at sea, the life jackets are literally life preservers.

1. If you were manufacturing life jackets to be used in an area where the possibility of puncturing an airfilled life jacket is too high, what kind of material would you use, and why would you choose that material over anything else?

2. Why are air or gas filled life jackets the ones most commonly found on aircraft but not so common for activities like pleasure boating or water skiing?

Activity #2 Creating a rainbow

Predict what **you** think will happen to the layers if the straw is turned upside down (with a finger covering the open end of the straw).

Have a group member invert the straw. What was the result? Why do **you** think this happened?

Activity #3 Don't judge a Coke can by its label!

Wilma and Margo are still puzzled as to what happened to that can of Coke. Write a letter to them explaining what happened and give them some practical advice when they go backpacking again.

Activity #4 Is it or is it not, pure gold?

Sometimes industry has the need for a material which is a result of 2 or more elements blended to make an alloy.

What do you hypothesize will be the density of an alloy? Will it be closer to the higher density, the lower density, between, or greater than the higher, or lower than the lowest density?

Test your hypothesis.

questions about their specific tasks. The questions were designed to determine if the students understood the activity and could apply the information to a real-life situation.

The second day, we held a "scientific convention" where each group presented its results. The class asked questions about the proposed hypothesis, the experiments, the results presented, and the assumptions made by the investigators. I was exhilarated. My students were actually *doing* science. The class generated a number of questions for each of the groups and discussed how the group might explore the questions. The variety of questions impressed me. One student asked, for instance, "Why did the Diet Coke have a different mass than the regular Coke? The label indicates that they have the same volume and the cans appear to be the same." The answers were equally impressive. "Maybe the Diet Coke has more gas in it than the regular Coke!" responded one student. "I always burp more when I drink Diet Coke." A third student volunteered her opinion: "I think sugar has a larger mass than NutraSweet. I want the next group to compare the mass of sugar and NutraSweet when they do the activity. I hope my group gets to do this tomorrow!"

Were these the same students who a few days before had refused to use the term "mass"? What was happening to them? They really wanted to figure out the difference between the Coke and Diet Coke. I would never have imagined that this question would be so engaging for them.

On the third day, the groups rotated and performed one of the other activities with the modified questions that had been generated by the class. The fourth day we continued the "scientific convention" to present the conclusions to the newly generated questions.

The activities had been a complete success, and the students were feeling good about how things were going. A few students shared their thoughts in their journal entries. "We should do all of our labs like this," they wrote, and "These activities really helped me understand what's going on in the class." I was thrilled at the responses, but I was concerned about the amount of time we had spent on the topic of density. Whereas I would normally spend only one 50-minute period on the

topic, I had already spent four class periods. The time commitments for using groupwork had definitely put a strain on my yearly timetable, but I was really thrilled that the students were thinking and solving problems in a more meaningful way. Concerned about the curriculum still to be covered, I decided to give a short quiz on density and then continue with the rest of the chapter.

The quiz was traditional in format (see Figure 4.2). It required students to calculate the density of a substance given its mass and volume by rearranging an equation and solving for the unknown variable. It also required them to interpret a data table. It was the same quiz I had always given for density.

I was astonished when I graded the quizzes. These students had not done any better on the test than had students from previous years. I was crushed. I really thought that the students had grasped the concept of density and would be able to apply it. I decided to discuss my disappointment with the students and solicit their input.

The next day I asked, "What did you find difficult about the quiz on density?" The class was unusually quiet. Finally, Marta raised her hand and said, "Our group had a great time doing the activities, and I believe that we had a good understanding of the idea. But the test didn't give us an opportunity to show what we had learned." Everyone was quick to agree with Marta's perspective.

I was still digesting Marta's comments when Carlos raised his hand. This student had never asked a question or raised his hand, so I called upon him immediately. In a very soft voice, Carlos explained: "The quiz was all math. I'm no good in math. I didn't think any of the questions were about the activities we did in class." I thanked the students for their honest responses and asked them to write test questions that they thought would have been more closely related to the activities.

I sat down at my desk, still amazed that the students had not made the connection between the activities and the key ideas of the units. They had participated in the activities and were very attentive when the important issues had come out in the "scientific convention." Two of the groups had actually demonstrated how to derive density

FIGURE 4.2. Two Tests: Traditional and Alternative

Chemistry Density Mini Quiz 1

Complete the table using the density equation that was discussed during our scientific convention. You are given two of the variables and asked to solve for the third variable. Please show all of your work in the space provided and include units with your final answers.

Substance	Mass (g)	Volume (ml)	Density (g/ml)
1. NaCl SHOW WORK:	74.3	27	——
2. HCl SHOW WORK:	——	96	.36
3. $MgBr_2$ SHOW WORK:	72.8	——	.64

4. What is the volume, in cubic centimeters, of a sample of cough syrup if it has a mass of 50.0 grams and a density of 0.950 g/cm^3?

5. What is the density of a shiny bar of metal weighing 57.3 grams and having a volume of 4.7 cm^3?

Chemistry Density Mini Quiz 2

Part 1: Use the attached pieces of binder paper to answer this section of the quiz. Select one of the following three alternatives:

1. Write a creative story to explain the concept of density. Imagine you are writing a story for a middle school student.

2. Compose a song that will convey the meaning of density and will explain how density is used in life.

3. Select a real life problem and use your knowledge of density to solve the problem. Explain how you would solve the problem.

Part 2: Please complete all of the problems below. Be sure to show all of your work and include units throughout the problem.

1. How large a container do you need to store 40 grams of a liquid that has a density of 2.0 grams per liter?

2. A copper penny has a mass of 3.1 grams and a volume of 0.35 cm^3. What is the density of copper?

3. A cube is 2 cm on each side. The density of the cube is 10.0 g/cm^3. What is its mass?

from mass and volume data. Yet despite their engagement and attentiveness, they were missing the key concepts. Was there something I should have done to help make the connections more explicit?

At the end of the period, the students turned in their proposed quizzes, which were quite surprising. All of the suggested questions were completely open-ended, and they represented a number of alternatives to evaluate student knowledge. One student suggested a creative story to explain the concept of density. Another would require that a song be written and sung to convey the information about density. A third idea was to take a real-life problem and solve it using the concept of density.

In general, the students selected nontraditional open-ended methods for evaluation. I had never really thought about traditional versus alternative evaluation before. I had tried to anticipate potential problems when the students had actually performed the activities, but I had not given much thought to how to evaluate. I had planned to use the individual reports, the group presentation grades, and the quiz grades to assess the effectiveness of the lessons.

Instead, I now decided to develop a new quiz that incorporated the students' suggested questions (see Figure 4.2). The students were asked to select one of the three possible questions, to complete some calculations, and to demonstrate their knowledge of density. Although the second set of quizzes was much more time consuming to grade, the results were remarkably better than the first. The grades were higher and the tests indicated that the students were able to calculate density and had a concrete understanding of a relatively abstract concept.

Why did the students do better on the second test? I speculated that the scores were higher because the students were able to express their understanding of the concept in methods most comfortable to them. To test my hypothesis, I asked the students to share their thoughts about the quiz in their daily journal entries. Megan wrote, "I really felt like you wanted to know my ideas instead of asking me to repeat what was taught." Juan commented, "It was really cool to be able

to use what I'm good at (writing) to do a science test." Greg felt that "the quiz was okay but I prefer the first quiz 'cause it was easier for me."

Why were the students able to perform the math calculations on the second test? I had never gone over the first test or showed them how to do the density calculations. Was it because they had seen them on the first test and felt more comfortable the second time around? Had they used their textbook as a reference to learn how to set up the problems? Was it a combination of things? I decided to include the second quiz grade with the other grades. I realized that I needed to carefully plan how I would evaluate groupwork lessons in the future.

A few days later, I was explaining what had happened to another teacher, who expressed shock that I had allowed the students to take an alternative test. I said, "I know it takes a lot more time and creativity, but I think that the students really appreciated being a part of the decision-making process and having a say in how they would be evaluated. I have really seen a change in their attitude about the class. They seem more confident and they appear to be making a greater effort in the course work." The other teacher looked at me and said, "You are doing a real disservice to your students. They need to be able to take standardized tests. If they want to go to college they have to be able to function in a traditional mode. No one is going to let them create a story or write a song. Think about their future!" Before I even had a chance to respond, the other teacher walked out.

I wanted to scream, but there was no one to hear me. My first reaction was to discredit my colleague. Who was this teacher, anyway? She didn't use groupwork as a part of her teaching, so how would she know about alternative evaluation?

But after I calmed down, her words began to penetrate. Although we had totally different philosophies about teaching and learning, I couldn't help but think about our conversation. Was I doing the students a disservice? Would alternative evaluation methods somehow hamper my students' ability to be successful on standardized exams? Is it important to match evaluation methods with teaching strategies?

NOTES

1. This case originally appeared in Shulman, Lotan, & Whitcomb, *Groupwork in Diverse Classrooms: A Casebook for Education,* (Teachers College Press, 1998).

2. Complex Instruction, developed at Stanford University, is a groupwork model that emphasizes the development of higher-order thinking skills in heterogeneous classrooms. It addresses issues of status that arise in small groups. See Cohen, *Designing Groupwork: Strategies for the Heterogeneous Classroom* (2nd ed.) (Teachers College Press, 1994).

A Waypoint on the Journey to Literacy

Marge Collins and Pat Dawson

It is 5:00 P.M. on a rainy Wednesday in March. We had been talking for an hour and a half without a break. Ten members of the district's Action Research Team—teachers, an associate superintendent, and an outside facilitator—intently faced one another. Usually, at this time of day, conversation lags; keys clink, ready for the car's ignition; eyes are riveted on the clock. This afternoon was different. The heated discussion raged on. "That's not fair! The student's overall portfolio level should not be determined by the lowest component score! Just because he has a spelling score of 3, he shouldn't be ranked at the early beginning level. His reading is a level 7 and his writing a level 4. How can he be ranked at early beginning level when he is reading at an independent level?" a teacher argued. The associate superintendent was adamant. "The overall score should be the lowest of the three component scores. That is the format used by the New Jersey school district, and it works well for them. We should follow their model." "How about using the average score? That would give equal weight to all the component scores," suggested another teacher. "That is meaningless," claimed a third teacher. "An average score would place him at a 5. That's advanced beginning. He didn't rank there for any component."

What were we to do?

Three years ago, our district began to focus on early literacy. One primary outcome mandated by the school board was that 90% of all students who had been in the district for three or more years would be reading at or above grade level by the end of third grade. "All students" included second language learners and students who had qualified for special education. In district parlance, this is known as a BHAG—a big, hairy, audacious goal. It was every bit of that and more.

One integral component of the early literacy program was the development of an assessment portfolio, containing specific measures of student progress (see Figures 5.1a and 5.1b). The portfolio was designed to provide a systematic, consistent, districtwide measure of a student's progress on the journey from emergent to independent reader and writer. Several times a year, the district collected data on the reading levels of first and second graders based on running records taken by the teacher. Those reading below the benchmark levels were considered "target" students. A number of questions arose from the data. Could teachers judge the level of a student's literacy simply from decoding books at benchmark reading levels? How did comprehension and fluency fit into the picture? There was other valuable information contained in the portfolio, such as writing samples and developmental spelling tests. How could we effectively use that information? Would the consideration of additional data change the level of a student's literacy achievement? Another issue that challenged the district administration and teacher leaders was how to best communicate this information to other teachers, parents, and the wider community. We felt that assessment taken on an individual basis

FIGURE 5.1A. Early Literacy Summary Sheet

Name _____ **Date of Birth** _____

Kindergarten

Teacher: _____

	Fall	Winter	Spring
Letter Names		—	
Letter Sounds	—		
Phonemic Awarenes		—	
Concepts of Print		—	
Writing Sample			
Emergent Reading Behaviors:			

(Book Levels 1, 2, 3)
Interventions student has received:

First Grade

Teacher: _____

	Fall		Winter	Spring	
Concepts of Print			—		—
Letter/Sound Identification					
Writing Vocabulary			—		
Sentence Dictation			—		
Word Test					
Writing Sample					
Gentry Spelling	—				
Running Record	Sept.	Nov.	Jan.	March	May

Interventions student has received:

Second Grade

Teacher: _____

	Fall		Winter	Spring	
Sentence Dictation			—		—
Word Test					
Writing Sample			—		
Gentry Spelling			—		
Running Record	Sept.	Nov.	Jan.	March	May

Fluent Independent Reader Test
Interventions student has received:

Third Grade

Teacher: _____

	Fall		Winter	Spring	
Sentence Dictation			—		
Running Record	Sept.	Nov.	Jan.	March	May
Fluent Independent Reader Test	Date Passed:			Score:	

Interventions student has received:

NB: Parent Surveys are a part of each student's portfolio.

FIGURE 5.1B. Early Literacy Assessment Portfolio Components

COMPONENT	WHICH STUDENTS	FREQUENCY
KINDERGARTEN		
Parent Survey	All	Fall
Letter Names	All	Fall/Spring
Letter Sounds	All	Winter/Spring
Phonemic Awareness	All	Fall/Spring
Concepts of Print	All	Fall/Spring
Writing Samples	All	Fall/Winter/Spring
Emergent Reading Behaviors Book Levels 1, 2, 3	All	By Spring
FIRST GRADE		
Parent Survey	All	Fall
Concepts of Print	All	Fall
Letter/Sound Identification	All Target	Fall Winter/Spring
Writing Vocabulary	All	Fall/Spring
Sentence Dictation	All Target	Fall Spring
Running Record	All	Sept./Nov./Jan./March/May
Word Test	All	Fall/Ongoing
Writing Sample	All	Fall/Winter/Spring
Gentry Spelling	All	Winter/Spring
SECOND GRADE		
Parent Survey	All	Fall
Sentence Dictation	All Target	Fall Spring
Running Record	All	Sept./Nov./Jan./March/May
Word Test	All	Fall Ongoing if needed
Writing Sample	All	Fall/Winter/Spring
Gentry Spelling	All	Fall/Winter/Spring
Fluent Independent Reader Test	Those likely to pass	Winter/Ongoing
THIRD GRADE		
Parent Survey	All	Fall
Sentence Dictation	All	Fall/Spring
Running Record	Target Others	Sept./Nov./Jan./March/May Oct.
Writing Sample	All	Pilot–TBA
Fluent Independent Reader Test	Target and New Students	When they are likely to pass

and over a long period of time would give an in-depth picture of a child's learning. The problem was compiling the data into one easily comprehensible score.

We thought we found the answer in a rubric that had been developed by a New Jersey school district, in conjunction with the Educational Testing Service. In essence, the rubric was a continuum of a child's literacy journey from the early emergent through the advanced independent level. Each level contained three components: reading, writing, and spelling. The classroom teacher used the rubric to score each child's portfolio, coming up with one composite score for each child. The lowest of the scores determined the student's literacy level.

Three teacher leaders (ourselves included) examined the New Jersey materials and, using their rubric as our model, developed an eight-point Reading/Writing Scale, coordinating the scale's points to the district's benchmarks in reading (see Figure 5.2). Twenty-three teachers, primarily K–2 teachers, piloted the portfolio scoring process. First, we scored four randomly selected portfolios of our own students and subsequently brought the scored portfolios to a calibration session at the district office. During the first phase of the calibration session, four sample portfolios, ranging from kindergarten through second grade, were scored by groups of four teachers. The scores were compared and discussed, leading to a group consensus on scoring criteria. There was general agreement on three of the portfolios. However, the fourth portfolio proved to be much more troublesome, sparking the animated discussion detailed earlier. There was general agreement about the student's scores in the varying components: reading level 7 (independent), writing level 4 (beginning), spelling level 3 (early beginning). However, we could not reach agreement on a composite score. Finally, the discussion was halted so the second phase of the calibration process could proceed. The resolution to this particular problem would have to wait. For today, we would use the score of the lowest component for the portfolio's composite score.

For the second phase of the calibration process, the teachers turned toward the piles of portfolios stacked on their tables. Pairs of teachers

eagerly set to work on their first portfolio. The room buzzed in animated discussion. Papers were strewn about the tables. Eyes darted between student work samples and the rubric descriptors. Everyone was talking at once. As soon as one portfolio was scored, hands reached out for the next. When told to stop, teachers exclaimed, "We're not finished!" The rubric scores were collected from each pair of teachers. The results were astounding! Out of 34 student portfolios scored, only two had a variance of 2 points between the score awarded by the classroom teacher and the calibrators; in all other cases the variance was 1 point or less. In 14 cases, there was an exact match between the score of the classroom teacher and the calibrators! The rubric worked! The teacher participants were enthusiastic. This had been fun!

At our next meeting, we had to come back to the thorny issue of deciding how to report student scores. For simplicity in reporting, administrators advocated for a single score for each student. Should we use the lowest component score, the median, the highest? The issue was complicated by the fact that the scores would be reported to multiple audiences: classroom teachers, schools, parents, the district administration, and the wider community. Each constituent would have a different interpretation of the scores, depending largely upon how informed each was about the district's literacy process. How could we disseminate this information in a way that would be meaningful to each group? One factor that concerned the teachers was giving equal weight to reading, writing, and spelling. Another concern was how students' scores would reflect upon them as teachers.

After extensive discussion, we decided that the best solution was to use the lowest component score as the composite score but include the subscores in reading and writing. The teachers were relieved. They could live with the lowest component score if the specific reading and writing levels also were included, demonstrating students' strengths and weaknesses.

We still were left with some unresolved issues. A number of questions about implementation arose. We discussed the difficulty of training all the kindergarten through second grade teachers so that they could begin using the rubric in the fall. How would we help teachers find time to add yet another assessment piece to their plate when they were *already* struggling to find the time to assess each of their students individually? There was also concern about how to deal with the different levels of teacher competency, particularly with new teachers who may have had little training in the district's "best teaching practices." Given the high turnover in staffing in recent years, how could we maintain consistency in the teaching and assessment of literacy, especially as the district focus moved to other areas of the curriculum?

Another major area of concern for administrators and teacher leaders was how the state standardized testing results would correlate with the portfolio assessment results. While we did not conduct a systematic comparison of the two sets of data, a preliminary analysis indicated that the results were close. The target students determined by the standardized test scores were the same students we had targeted through the portfolio assessments. What concerns us now is using all these data to make a difference—tailoring our instruction so that we help the target students substantially improve their reading, writing, and spelling. In addition, how do we help parents and the general public understand the value of using *both* standardized and portfolio assessments? How can we explain that the standardized tests show how the students did at one point on one day, while the portfolio assessment offers a broader-based, long-term indicator of a child's journey in literacy? Can we convince the public that standardized test scores should not be taken as finite measures of a student's worth, but rather as indicators of a waypoint on the long road to becoming a literate individual?

There are so many questions and a sense of so little time to resolve them. Our journey with literacy and assessment continues.

FIGURE 5.2. Primary Reading/Writing Scale: Development of Children's Strategies for Making Sense of Print

Literacy Scales: Scoring Form	Grade: K 1 2 3
Child's Name: _____	Date: _____

1—EARLY EMERGENT*

Student displays an awareness of some conventions of reading, such as the front/back of books and the distinctions between print and pictures. S/he sees the construction of meaning from text as "magical" or exterior to the print. While the child may be interested in the contents of books, there is as yet little apparent attention to turning written marks into language. Child is beginning to notice environmental print. S/he uses meaning and structure for pretend reading. S/he has a beginning sense of one-to-one correspondence.

Reading Level: B-3
Gentry Spelling Level: 1.0–1.5 Precommunicative
Writing Sample: Student uses letters in writing, sometimes in random or scribble fashion. Letters often do not correspond to sounds.

2—EMERGENT*

Student engages in pretend reading and writing. S/he uses reading-like ways that clearly approximate book language. S/he demonstrates a sense of the story being "read," using picture clues and recall of storyline. S/he may draw upon predictable language patterns in anticipating and recalling the story. S/he has a sense of one-to-one correspondence.

Reading Level: 4–6
Gentry Spelling Level: 2.0 Semiphonetic
Writing Sample: Student uses letters in writing. S/he uses beginning and/or ending sounds.

3—EARLY BEGINNING*

Student really reads. S/he understands one-to-one correspondence and the concept of word. S/he predicts actively in new material, using syntax and story line. A small stable sight vocabulary is becoming established.

Reading Level: 7–10
Gentry Spelling Level: 2.5 Semiphonetic/Phonetic
Writing Sample: Student shows awareness of beginning and ending sounds, especially in temporary spelling. S/he begins to use word boundaries. Sentence structure is simple and repetitive.

4—BEGINNING*

Student shows awareness of beginning and ending sounds. S/he is beginning to pay attention to medial sounds. S/he is beginning to use the cueing systems and to self-correct and self-monitor. S/he uses sight vocabulary words.

Reading Level: 11–12
Gentry Spelling Level: 3.0 Phonetic
Writing Sample: Student is using beginning and ending sounds and is beginning to use letter patterns. S/he is able to express his/her thoughts in a few sentences.

FIGURE 5.2. (*continued*)

5—ADVANCED BEGINNING*

Student draws on the major cueing systems. S/he self-corrects and identifies words through the use of letter-sound patterns. S/he has a sense of story or syntax. Reading new material requires considerable effort and support.

Reading Level: 13–16
Gentry Spelling Level: 3.5 Phonetic/Transitional
Writing Sample: Writing and spelling reveal awareness of letter patterns. Conventions of writing such as capitalization and full stops are beginning to appear but are not consistent. S/he is capable of producing longer, more meaningful text.

6—EARLY INDEPENDENT*

Student handles familiar text on his/her own, but still needs some support with unfamiliar material. S/he figures out words and self-corrects by drawing on a combination of letter-sound relationships, word structure, story line and syntax. Strategies of re-reading and making inferences from larger chunks of text to determine the meaning of unknown words are becoming established. S/he has a large stable sight vocabulary.

Reading Level: 17–20
Gentry Spelling Level: 4.0 Transitional
Writing Sample: Student shows evidence that conventions of writing are becoming more consistent. Writing continues to lengthen, increase in meaning, and show more organization. Students begin to use descriptive vocabulary.

7—INDEPENDENT*

Student handles unfamiliar material without support. S/he figures out words and self-corrects, using multiple strategies. Strategies of re-reading and making inferences from larger chunks of text to determine the meaning of an unknown word are well established. S/he begins to use higher level of thinking skills in interpreting text.

Reading Level: 21–22
Gentry Spelling Level: 4.5 Transitional/Conventional
Writing Sample: Student begins to write independently. Writing increases in originality and organization. S/he begins to write in a variety of genres. Consistency in the use of conventions continues to increase.
Fluent Independent Reader Test:

8—ADVANCED INDEPENDENT*

Student reads independently, using multiple strategies flexibly. S/he monitors and self-corrects for meaning. S/he uses higher level thinking skills in interpreting texts from a variety of genres.

Reading Level: 24+
Gentry Spelling Level: 5.0 Conventional
Writing Sample: Student writes independently in a variety of genres, with originality and organization. S/he has the conventions of print under control.

*N.B.: Also refer to the other elements in the Early Literacy Portfolio to inform your sense of the student's stage on this scale.

Figure is based on rating scale developed by South Brunswick, New Jersey, teachers and ETS staff.

CASE 6

A Rubric for Reading Fluency

Carol Glenn

"Hey, Debbie, can I borrow the stopwatch?"

Debbie, a fellow seventh-grade language arts/social studies teacher, and I have worked together for five years at West Shore Middle School.

"Sure, but can I have it back by Thursday? I need to do the makeups."

"I'll have it back to you by Wednesday. I can't imagine the reading fluency assessments will take more than a couple of days."

"Well, let me know how it goes."

The language arts team at West Shore Middle School has worked for a year to develop and implement meaningful multiple assessments to determine if our students are working at standard. Two years ago we reviewed and discussed the California State Standards (available at www.cde.ca.gov), adopted our own, and set into motion the development of a Standards and Assessment binder containing the multiple assessments each grade level team had collaboratively created. Our goal this year was to pilot these documents.

I was surprised at my own apprehension when it came time for me to implement the reading fluency portion of these assessments. Although I'd always had students read to me, I'd never been asked to do it so formally. To prepare myself for this task, I'd attended the reading association meetings and discussed at length with my curriculum director the value of a reading fluency assessment at the middle school level. I was informed and convinced that reading 150 words per minute on a grade level passage was the standard and that the data supporting the link between reading flu-ency and comprehension were valid. Why was I nervous? I had read the instructions, copied the passages, practiced on colleagues, secured a stopwatch, and was ready to go.

I asked Kristy, a seventh-grade student in my language arts/social studies core class and a gradu-ate of my remedial reading class the previous year, if she'd be willing to start the process with me. I shared with her the objective of the assessment: to determine her reading fluency and level of comprehension. It felt safe starting with her be-cause of the relationship we had developed in my reading class. She was familiar with the traits of good/effective readers: reading more than one word at a time, reading the punctuation, using intonation, self-correcting and reading from line to line smoothly. A good place to start? I was set-ting myself up for success!

I followed the instructions meticulously. Kristy preread the passage to focus her attention. That seemed fair. When her body language indicated she was done, I picked up the bright yellow stop-watch and asked her if she was ready. A minute later we were done. Why had I been so nervous?

"All right, Kristy, 138!"

A quizzical look.

"150 is standard. You'll be there by spring!"

Another quizzical look.

"Did I pass, Ms. Glenn?"

It was my turn to look quizzical. For a student who had taken so many academic risks the previ-ous year, working so hard to improve her reading, this assessment seemed to confuse her. I asked her how she felt about the process and her response, in hindsight, seems obvious. She had no idea why I was "testing" her fluency in this manner. We'd never done this type of thing before. The activities we did in the reading class to improve her fluency centered on read-alouds, reader's theater, paired readings, and book clubs. Because I had never timed how fast she could read, she wasn't sure what I wanted her to do. In an attempt to "pass" the timed test—and, I think, to impress me—she read through all of the punctuation, did not self-correct, and stumbled over words that would not normally cause her trouble.

Well, at least this assessment had a comprehension component that would allow Kristy to be successful. I was confident that the simple four-point scale (see bottom of Figure 6.1) provided me with an adequate tool to determine Kristy's comprehension.

"OK, Kristy, tell me what the passage was about."

Her silence and furrowed brows spoke volumes. After a little coaxing Kristy was able to recall the main character, part of the setting and a few important details. I looked at the four-point scale and was stumped. It felt so subjective! I gave her a 2 because I had 29 other assessments to give and had to get the stopwatch back to Debbie in two days. Did it really matter anyway? The scale only told me if she had done well or not. I needed something more concrete to tell her and to guide my further instruction.

I tried to reassure her, and myself, that she had done well. Unfortunately, she was just the first of many students who hadn't self-corrected, read the punctuation, used intonation, visualized the setting, related to the character, or followed the plot. I tried to hide my disappointment, but I'm sure my lack of enthusiasm and genuine praise was evident. Why hadn't the students demonstrated the *fluency*: the self-correction, reading phrases instead of words, and pacing with the proper intonation we'd worked so hard to master? Where should I go from here? The comprehension rubric gave me just as little information to guide my practice as the fluency rubric had offered. Why was it that so many students were unable to recall the basic plot and conflict so clearly present in the passage?

The answers to those questions would have to wait. I had assessments to give, lessons to plan, and papers to correct.

I returned the stopwatch to Debbie on Wednesday.

"So . . . how'd it go?"

"Awful!" I responded. "Very few students demonstrated *my* understanding of fluency."

"What were you expecting?"

"Well, I thought the students would self-correct, sound out words using the word study strategies we've been doing, and at least stop at the punctuation. You'd think this was a speed-reading contest."

"How'd they do on the comprehension component?"

"Just as poorly. Most of the students scored a 1 or 2, but I think it is way too subjective. I'm so disappointed."

Debbie continued to ask me questions that helped me articulate my experience, frustration and disappointment. At the end of the conversation I was able to see more clearly why I was so frustrated. I'd asked students to perform on demand instead of demonstrate what they are capable of doing, and had to use rubrics that did not match the objective of gaining more information to guide curriculum.

The relief I felt at having had a trusted colleague to "coach" me through this experience gave me the confidence to go public. At our next department meeting I mentioned my experience with the reading fluency/comprehension assessment and found that I was not alone. Instead of addressing the assessment, the discussion centered on the daily evidence of reading fluency we'd experienced in our classrooms. The students were connecting with the text, relating to the characters, visualizing the setting, discussing the conflicts, questioning their comprehension and new vocabulary, self-correcting, and reading the punctuation with the proper intonation and enunciation. Well, not every student, but enough anecdotal evidence was shared to convince me that I was on the right track. So, what was wrong? Why hadn't our students "passed" the reading fluency and comprehension assessment?

FIGURE 6.1. Comprehension and Fluency Assessment: Teacher Recording Sheet

Name of Child: _____   Date: _____   Grade: ___7___

Man Overboard

A sharp sound startled him. Somewhere, off in the blackness, someone had fired a gun three	16
times.	17
Rainsford sprang up and moved quickly to the rail, mystified. He strained his eyes in the di-	33
rection from which the reports had come, but it was like trying to see through a blanket. He leaped	52
up onto the rail and balanced himself there to get a greater elevation: his pipe, striking a rope, was	71
knocked from his mouth. He lunged for it. A short, hoarse cry came from his lips as he realized he	91
had reached too far and had fallen overboard. The cry was punched off as the blood-warm waters	109
of the Caribbean Sea closed over his head.	117
He struggled up to the surface and tried to cry for help, but the wash from the speeding yacht	136
slapped him in the face. The salty water in his open mouth gagged and strangled him. Desperately	153
he struck out with strong strokes after the receding lights of the yacht, but he stopped before he	171
had covered fifty feet. He calmed down and assessed his situation. It was not the first time he had	191
been in a tough situation. There was a chance that his cries could be heard by someone aboard the	210
yacht. But the chance was slim and grew much slimmer as the yacht continued on. He shouted with	228
all his might. The lights of the yacht became faint, looking like ever-vanishing fireflies. Then they	245
were blotted out entirely by the black night.	253

Retell/Comprehension:

4   Excellent
3   Satisfactory, and adequate understanding
2   Some understanding
1   Very little understanding

_____ WPM – Errors = _____
or
_____ WPM – Errors = _____
) 15000

Fluency:

3   Reads fluently with expression, reads the punctuation
2   Reads primarily in phrases, little intonation, ignores some punctuation
1   Primarily word-by-word reading

FIGURE 6.2. Fluency Rubric

5/6—Fluent reader

- reads punctuation
- varies voice/intonation
- self-corrects
- reads in phrases
- uses appropriate speed/pace – varies it effectively
- moves from line to line smoothly

4—Standard reader

- reads punctuation a majority of the time (50% or more)
- uses some variation in voice/intonation
- self-corrects a majority of the time (50% or more)
- reads two or more words at a time
- uses a comfortable speed/pace but lacks variety
- moves from line to line

2/3—Developing reader

- attempts to read punctuation
- occasionally varies voice/intonation
- attempts to self-correct but needs prompting
- attempts to read more than one word at a time
- attempts to read at a comfortable speed/pace
- hesitates between lines

1—Struggling reader

- does not read punctuation
- uses a monotone
- does not self-correct
- reads one word at a time
- moves from line to line awkwardly

EPILOGUE

After assessing 90 students using the materials I had been given, it became clear to me that the four-point scales we were asked to use to determine a student's fluency and comprehension were insufficient. An articulated rubric that could be used in the classroom to teach students the qualities of fluency and comprehension was needed. It seemed unfair to me to assess students using criteria that had never been shared with them. No wonder, when they saw the stopwatch, that they thought the person who read the most was the "winner."

Figures 6.1, 6.2, and 6.3 include very rough drafts of what my colleagues and I are using this fall to assess a student's fluency and comprehension. Our goal is to pilot the rough outlines we created, ask for student input, and redesign the rubrics so they can be used as teaching and assessment tools. I feel no professional conflict in *teaching to the test*; instead, I feel that my practice will be more clearly articulated and the people who I am teaching will be given the skills they need to be competent readers.

FIGURE 6.3. Reading Comprehension Rubric

6—a student retells the story thoroughly and clearly
- all elements of a story are included without prompting:
   - characterization
   - plot sequence
   - setting
   - point of view
   - theme—if appropriate
   - conflict—if appropriate
   - tone—if appropriate
- details are accurate
- makes a connection between title and text

5—a student retells the story well
- a minimum of three elements of a story are included without prompting:
   - characterization
   - plot sequence
   - setting
   - point of view
   - theme—if appropriate
   - conflict—if appropriate
   - tone—if appropriate
- details are accurate

4—a student is able to retell the story clearly
- a minimum of three elements of a story are included with minimal prompting:
   - characterization
   - plot sequence
   - setting
   - point of view
   - theme—if appropriate
   - conflict—if appropriate
   - tone—if appropriate
- details are accurate

3—a student retells the story
- a minimum of three elements of a story are included with some prompting:
   - characterization
   - plot sequence
   - setting
   - point of view
   - theme—if appropriate
   - conflict—if appropriate
   - tone—if appropriate
- very few details are included

2—a student has difficulty retelling the story
- two of the elements of the story are included with some prompting
- details are omitted

1—a student is unable to retell the story without prompting

0—a student is unable to retell the story

CASE 7

Assessment for Assessment's Sake?

Christina Carmelich

After three years of working on a district committee to develop standards-based assessments, I thought I understood how to incorporate standards and assessments into my curriculum. But after developing a major interdisciplinary unit that incorporated technology, I now have many more questions about assessment than I did before. For example, how many new assessments should I develop? How do the assessments capture what my students have learned? How important is it to involve students in the development of rubrics? And where do teachers get the time to do all of the assessments required in a standards-based program?

I've been teaching sixth grade at an ethnically diverse elementary school in San Jose, California, for seven years. One of the things I've always loved about teaching sixth grade has been introducing students to the topic of heritage. The sixth grade social studies book I use begins with a chapter on immigration as a way to enter into ancient history studies. Over the years, I've found that most of my students enter sixth grade with the beliefs that they have little personal connection to other countries and that their ancestors were born and raised in America. I've delighted in helping my students research their heritage and realize that the United States is a "melting pot" composed of people from all cultures of the world.

In the past, I taught my students about heritage through a two-week social studies unit that included the making of a class quilt. By working together to create a quilt, students in my class gained an appreciation of each individual's back-

ground and learned that their families came from a wide range of countries and cultures. (The student population at my school reflected the diversity of the surrounding community: 40% Latino, 30% European, 20% Asian, 7% Arabic, and 3% African American.) To assess student learning about heritage, I relied upon the end-of-chapter test from the sixth-grade textbook.

Last summer, I participated in an intensive summer institute sponsored by Joint Venture: Silicon Valley Network, a major education reform initiative funded heavily by corporations in the region. The summer institute focused on project-based learning using multimedia and encouraged teachers to implement student-centered classroom projects that incorporated technology. The summer institute also emphasized the need for multiple measures of student results, a concept consistent with my district assessment work. In discussion with other summer institute participants, I decided to incorporate the project-based learning and multimedia concepts into my heritage unit. When I returned to my classroom in the fall, I eagerly introduced the expanded heritage unit to my students. The unit had five components:

Heritage stories. Each student began by researching his or her heritage through interviewing relatives and then wrote a narrative about his or her ancestry. I evaluated the stories using three tools—a district writing rubric that I adapted with my students, a rubric for peer editing, and an editing checklist (see Figures 7.1, 7.2, 7.3).

FIGURE 7.1. Scoring Rubrics for Heritage Story 1998

SCORE LEVELS	DESCRIPTION
6	**SUPERIOR PERFORMANCE** • Presents superior thought-provoking ideas. • Not only easy to follow but exceeds writing to understand. Reader gets involved with the story content. • Organization is well connected with words and phrases. • Directly answers prompt. • Uses several quotes and adds similes to show understanding.
5	**GOOD PERFORMANCE** • Presents good thoughts and ideas. • Easily understood. Ideas are connected and flow without breaks. • Clear sense of organization. There are one or two phrases. • Is related to prompt. • Uses a few quotes or details to develop the ideas and understanding. • Uses some complex sentences. • Shows good command of conventions, vocabulary, spelling, grammar and punctuation with only one or two errors.
4	**EFFECTIVE WRITING PERFORMANCE** • Presents an interesting and thoughtful idea. • Understanding is easy, with ideas connected, and there is no serious break in flow. • Effectively organized with some connected phrases. • Is related to prompt. • Uses some quotes and details to develop that the idea is understood. • Uses some complex sentence structure. • Shows general command of conventions, vocabulary, spelling, grammar and punctuation with infrequent errors.
3	**COMPETENT WRITING PERFORMANCE** • Story is understandable, but not always easy and smooth to read. • Contains mostly obvious ideas. There is little that is new or that a reader would not expect. • Shows some sense of organization, with some unevenly developed ideas. The conclusion may be simply tacked on. • It is directly related to part or all of the prompt or an extension of the prompt. • Contains some reasons, details and examples. May have some incomplete explanations. • Uses simplistic and ordinary sentence structure. • Shows basic command of vocabulary, grammar, spelling, conventions and punctuation with an occasional error which does not interfere with the writer's message.
2	**BASIC WRITING PERFORMANCE** • Contains ideas which seem to jump around and are not closely connected. • Contains simple, thinly developed statements of the topic with some unclear explanations. • Shows simple sense of organization. • May contain ideas with little or no relationship to the prompt or may simply paraphrase the prompt. • May have rambling sentences or fragments and simple vocabulary and structure. • Contains frequent errors in grammar, spelling, conventions and/or punctuation, which may interfere with the writer's message.
1	**MINIMAL WRITING PERFORMANCE** • Work is extremely difficult to understand: may be brief, confusing, illogical. • May be simple restatement of the prompt with a listing of ideas or details. • Shows little or no sense of organization. • Has confused sentence structure. • Contains numerous errors in grammar, spelling, conventions and/or punctuation.

FIGURE 7.2. Peer Editing Rubric

INTRODUCTION:										
Does it have an interesting or catchy title?	1	2	3							
Does the introduction create suspense or interest?	1	2	3	4	5					
Is it clear what the problem will be?	1	2	3	4	5					
BODY PARAGRAPHS:										
Do the supporting paragraphs draw a picture in your mind?	1	2	3	4	5	6	7	8	9	10
Does it seem like it comes alive for the reader?	1	2	3	4	5					
CONCLUSION:										
Does the conclusion make the reader wish there was more to read?	1	2	3	4	5					
MECHANICS:										
Is the punctuation clear & without error?	1	2	3	4	5					
PREPARATION/ORGANIZATION:										
Is it typed or neatly written and double-spaced?	1	2	3	4						
Is the rough draft included?	1	2	3	4						
Is the outline complete?	1	2	3	4						
Are there at least 5 sources?	1	2	3							
Are there two student reviews written by classmates?	1	2								
TOTAL:	_____/50									

FIGURE 7.3. Editing Checklist

Writer's Name_____

Editor's Name_____

Check the draft for the following:

1. Composition has a beginning, middle and end.

2. Composition holds the reader's interest and makes sense.

3. Paragraphs often have a topic and ending sentence.

4. Sentences are complete thoughts.

5. Sentences do not begin with AND or BECAUSE.

6. Interesting words are used – evidence of a thesaurus.

7. Spelling is correct – evidence of a dictionary.

8. There is a good conclusion.

Check the final copy for the following:

1. Sentences begin with capital letters – end with punctuation.

2. Paragraphs are indented.

3. The paper is neat and easily readable.

4. Writer used blue or black ink and cursive writing.

5. Margins on both sides of the paper.

6. Correct heading? One side of paper used?

Country reports. Each student conducted research on the Internet and composed a word-processed report on his or her country(ies) of origin. I graded the reports using the district writing rubric (see Figure 7.4) and made sure that students met the multimedia criteria.

The quilt. Each student completed a nine-block square to contribute to the class quilt. Students had to measure their blocks, translate aspects of their heritage onto five of the nine blocks, sew the nine pieces together, iron the block, and attach their square to that of another student. For the first time, I decided to assess each student's work on the quilt. I engaged the class in determining the criteria for assessing the quilt, asking questions like, "What would the best quilt look like?" We went from there.

Journals. Students also wrote daily in their journals about their reflections on the unit. Some of the typical questions I asked them to answer were "Where am I in the project?" and "What goals do I have for this week?" I assessed the journal entries according to a quick coding scheme I developed: four paragraphs were an A, three a B, two a C, and one a D.

Movies. The unit culminated in the creation of short movies about heritage. I divided my students into teams of four and gave them the option of creating their movie using one of five software programs. One of the teams participated in a multimedia fair organized by Joint Venture: Silicon Valley Network and had their movie evaluated by a panel of judges. For the other teams, I gave an A if the movie was complete and an F if it was incomplete. All of the students also presented their movies in an oral presentation, which I did not grade.

The expanded heritage unit rapidly consumed all of my time. I spent many hours deliberating over how to effectively integrate language arts, social studies, math, art, and multimedia into one unit. I felt I needed to create or find appropriate assessment tools for each component of the project. I also had a lot more student work to assess. As we moved into the moviemaking phase of the unit, I found that most of my evenings and weekends were devoted to working with students, figuring out the software programs and developing the movies. By then, the project had grown far longer than the original two-week unit, and I was beginning to see myself as the rabbit in *Alice in Wonderland* ("I'm late . . . I'm late . . . I must be on my way. I'm late . . . I'm late . . ."). I needed to get to other units. I was growing anxious to wrap up the movies and move on.

The movies were finally completed in the spring. I breathed a major sigh of relief! We finished the unit! There was a lingering doubt as I lay in bed at night, however. My district and the Joint Venture: Silicon Valley Network had drilled into my head the need to measure student results. I was feeling guilty about my cursory assessment of the student movies, especially given how much time we had spent making them. From experience, I knew that my students produced higher-quality work when they were involved in constructing their assessments, but I just didn't have the time or energy to develop yet another rubric with my class. Joint Venture: Silicon Valley Network had created a rubric for judges to use during the multimedia fair (see Figure 7.5), but I couldn't share it with my students because it wasn't written in "kid-friendly" language.

My head then began spinning as I reflected on the entire heritage unit. I had assessed the heritage stories, working with my students to adapt the district writing rubric. I had graded the students' country reports. I had engaged my kids in a conversation about what a good quilt looked like and then evaluated each student's quilt work. I had read and evaluated hundreds of journal entries. I had assessed—albeit quickly—the student movies. In sum, I had a lot of data in my gradebook and had a good sense of how my students were doing. But had I lost sight of my "big picture" goals as I focused on all the details? Did my students have a much deeper understanding of heritage and immigration than my former students did? Did they get excited about social studies? Were they more collaborative? Were they more technologically proficient?

And to what extent did the assessment results inform my instruction? I felt as if I hadn't had enough time to reflect on all the information I was collecting, as I was too busy racing from project component to project component, from one assessment to the next. One of the biggest challenges of the teaching profession is the lack of time to reflect on what one is doing and learning, and I had cut into the minimal reflection time I had by focusing on designing assessment tools and figuring out movie software programs. Would I have been a more effective, responsive teacher if I had only done one or two assessments during the unit, or would I—and my students—have lost something? Now that I have the assessment in place, will this unit be easier next year?

A recurring question loomed over me: Was I assessing just for the sake of assessment? Maybe I had let the pressure to measure student results get the best of me, at the expense of more instructional time and at the expense of my sanity. With all of these student results at my fingertips, could I easily conclude that my students' overall performance met my expectations . . . and the district's expectations? And what about those "intangibles" such as student engagement and motivation? I sensed that my students loved the unit and had gained in-depth knowledge, but would any of that enthusiasm and learning translate into high test scores on the statewide standardized test? At the end of the day, that's the most important assessment . . . or is it?

On the last day of the school year, a fifth grader named Larry ran up to me. "Mrs. C! Mrs. C! Am I going to be in your class next year? I want to do the heritage project!" he exclaimed. I sighed and didn't know what to say.

FIGURE 7.4. Language Arts Curriculum and Performance Standards: Writing

Students skilled in writing clearly understand their **purpose for writing**, have a well developed **process for writing** and a command of the **convention of writing**.

Purpose of Writing • Write for more than one purpose with guidance • Show interest in a variety of genres (writing such as literature and poetry) as models for writing • Recognize that writing represents thinking and speaking	**Purpose of Writing** • Write to express ideas, record information, and communicate with others with some guidance • Begin to understand a variety of writing styles and start to explore the writing domain • Communicate appropriately with family, friends and peers	**Purpose of Writing** • Explore the purpose of their own writing • Write in four domains (firsthand biography, autobiographical incident, report of information, story) • Recognize language appropriate to different audiences and communicate readily with family, friend and peers
Process of Writing • Plan what to write and use illustrations which follow the text • Provide content using teacher directed format (frame writing) • Use classroom resources • Begin to understand fiction • Dictate what they learn from story • Choose vocabulary to complete a sentence frame • Use a variety of visuals and three dimensional objects to share ideas (e.g. pictures, artifacts, diagrams) • Revise in response to suggestions from teacher or peers	**Process of Writing** • Use writing to explore or organize ideas when assisted by teacher and contribute to and make use of pre-writing activities • Provide sufficient information and detail to be understood when writing to an audience • Generate ideas that go beyond models provided in class • Begin to compare and contrast characters and ideas in writing • Translate the author's message into their own words • Choose simple vocabulary to make writing more interesting • Explore the use of technology to present ideas using writing, visuals, drawing and graphs • Revise work independently to order or expand writing	**Process of Writing** • Experiment with standard formats, using mapping, outlining and brainstorming techniques for prewriting • Provide appropriate facts and details from a variety of sources to develop the subject in some depth • Generate ideas in the form of opinions which are supported by literary text • Provide some inferences and evaluations of facts and details to make meaning for the reader • Gain facility of one aspect of an issue and consider other aspects of that issue • Vary vocabulary and begin to experiment with figurative language • Use introductory skills on a word processor along with other technology to present ideas • Begin to edit peers work as well as their own
Conventions of Writing • Use temporary spelling • Use simple nouns, pronouns, and verbs • Experiment with capitals and end line punctuation in simple sentences • Sequence sentences to tell a story	**Conventions of Writing** • Use correct spelling for common one and two syllable words • Use a variety of parts of speech and verb tenses with some accuracy • Use end line punctuation in simple sentences and experiment with internal punctuation • Use a few simple transitions	**Conventions of Writing** • Spell common vocabulary words accurately • Use simple sentences with short phrases with few grammatical errors • Use both end line and internal punctuation in complex sentences • Use a variety of simple transitions

Each of the six stages in these rubrics represents the highest performance moving along the K– 2 continuum. The expectation is that teams of teachers (and students) will create sub-sets of the standards adopted to focus more clearly on instruction at each level.

FIGURE 7.4. (*continued*)

Purpose of Writing	**Purpose of Writing**	**Purpose of Writing**
• Explore the purpose of their own writing and state the purpose adequately with occasional prompting	• Incorporate a clear and adequate statement of purpose	• Incorporate a clear and effective statement of purpose
• Write in eight domains (firsthand biography, autobiographical incident, report of information, story, problem solution, evaluation, cause and effect, observational)	• Write with skill in a variety of domains including resume, summary, reflective, persuasive, narrative, technical and scientific	• Demonstrate high level of skill in a broad variety of literary genres including resume, summary, reflective, persuasive, narrative, technical, and scientific and demonstrate mastery of one or two of these forms of writing
• Demonstrate some sense of audience	• Demonstrate a strong sense of audience with audiences of varied age, gender and ethnicity	• Demonstrate an exemplary sense of audience with most audiences regardless of age, gender or ethnicity
Process of Writing	**Process of Writing**	**Process of Writing**
• Organize using standard format of introductory paragraph, supporting paragraph, and concluding paragraph, with consistency	• Organize information to maintain logic and meaning	• Organize complex, specialized information to maintain logic and create coherence and unity
• Provide appropriate facts and details from a variety of sources to develop a subject in depth	• Provide appropriate factual and conceptual knowledge to develop the subject in depth	• Use an extensive base of factual and conceptual knowledge and an in-depth, sustained study of the topic to develop the subject
• Generate and expand ideas using examples from literary text	• Generate varied, creative writing using a variety of resources	• Generate varied and creative ideas for writing, capitalizing on the broadest variety of accessing and managing skills
• Make inferences and evaluations of facts and details to make meaning for the reader	• Make inferences from facts and conceptual knowledge and support them with appropriate fact and detail	• Make insightful inferences and support them with appropriate, highly specific detail
• Begin to recognize the possibility of using different aspects of issues in writing	• Demonstrate an awareness of multiple aspects of an issue and use these to write effectively	• Demonstrate a thorough awareness of multiple aspects of an issue and use writing judiciously and persuasively
• Vary vocabulary and choose words which reflect their beginning understanding of the nuances and subtleties of language	• Exhibit personal style and quality throughout most of the work, understanding the nuances and subtleties of language and choosing words for best expression from a broadening vocabulary	• Sustain personal style and quality throughout, using rich, precise and highly specialized vocabulary both subtly and persuasively
• Begin to use multimedia as a part of the learning process for conveying information	• Use skills in basic technology and multimedia to facilitate writing and to aide in communication and use visual aids such as graphs and charts to support writing	• Use technology and multimedia with skill to enhance communication and integrate appropriate visuals such as graphs and charts to clarify and support writing
• Begin to see peers as a resource for editing/revising	• Accept the editing of their peers and demonstrate skills in editing and revising own work	• Revise and edit own and others writing with skill, flexibility and experience
Conventions of Writing	**Conventions of Writing**	**Conventions of Writing**
• Can spell most common multi-syllable words	• Use resources to ensure accurate spelling of a rich vocabulary of words	• Spell accurately using a rich and highly specialized vocabulary
• Use simple and compound sentences with few grammatical errors and experiment with complex sentences	• Experiment with simple, compound, complex and compound-complex sentences and exhibit few grammatical errors	• Use a wide variety of sentence structures to enhance writing and have command of grammar
• Perfect punctuation of clauses and employ conventional mechanics and paragraphing	• Employ conventional mechanics and paragraphing with accuracy	• Write using broadest range of punctuation and paragraphing conventions with accuracy
• Use a variety of simple transitions effectively and experiment with other transitions	• Use transitions to develop logical flow of ideas	• Use transitions skillfully to achieve a natural flow of ideas

FIGURE 7.5. Multimedia Project Scoring Rubric: Scoring Guidelines

SCORE LEVELS	MULTIMEDIA *The integration of media objects such as text, graphics, video, animation, and sound to represent and convey information. Videotapes which include sound and images fit this definition.*	SCORE LEVELS	CONTENT *The topics, ideas, concepts, knowledge, and opinions that constitute the substance of the presentation.*	SCORE LEVELS	COLLABORATION *Working together jointly to accomplish a common intellectual purpose in a manner superior to what might have been accomplished working alone.*
5	Students have used multimedia in creative and effective ways that explore the particular strengths of the chosen format. All elements make a contribution. There are few technical problems and none of a serious nature.	**5**	Meets all criteria of the previous level and one or more of the following: • Reflects broad research • Application of critical thinking skills • Shows notable insight or understanding of the topic • Compels the audience's attention	**5**	Students were a very effective team. Division of responsibilities capitalized on the strengths of each team member. The final product was shaped by all members and represents something that would not have been possible to accomplish working alone.
4	Presentation blends 3 or more multimedia elements in an attractive, easy to follow format. With minor exceptions, all elements contribute rather than detract from the presentation's overall effectiveness.	**4**	The project has a clear goal related to a significant topic or issue. Information included has been compiled from several relevant sources. The project is useful to an audience beyond the students who created it.	**4**	Students worked together as a team on all aspects of the project. There was an effort to assign roles based on the skills/talents of individual members. All members strove to fulfill their responsibilities.
3	Presentation uses 2 or more media. There are some technical problems, but the viewer is able to follow the presentation with few difficulties.	**3**	The project presents information in an accurate and organized manner that can be understood by the intended audience. There is a focus that is maintained throughout the piece.	**3**	Students worked together on the project as a team with defined roles to play. Most members fulfilled their responsibilities. Disagreements were resolved or managed productively.
2	Presentation uses 2 or more media, but technical difficulties seriously interfere with the viewers' ability to see, hear or understand the content.	**2**	The project has a focus, but may stray from it at times. There is an organized structure, though it may not be carried through consistently. There may be factual errors or inconsistencies, but they are relatively minor.	**2**	Presentation is the result of a group effort, but only some members of the group contributed. There is evidence of poor communication, unresolved conflicts, or failure to collaborate on important aspects of the work.
1	Multimedia is absent from the presentation.	**1**	Project seems haphazard, hurried or unfinished. There are significant factual errors, misconceptions, or misunderstandings.	**1**	Presentation was created by one student working more or less alone (though may have received guidance or help from others).
MULTIMEDIA SCORE		**CONTENT SCORE**		**COLLABORATION SCORE**	

Adapted from Challenge 2000 Multimedia Project, R.Stites and M.Simkins.

CHAPTER 3

Using Assessments to Guide Instruction

A standards-based classroom supports the full integration of curriculum, instruction, and assessment. Such integration means that assessments are embedded in instruction; matched to the goals, formats, and processes of instruction; and provide ongoing learning experiences for students day-to-day. These links provide teachers with ongoing or "formative" assessment data and results that enable them to diagnose potential stumbling blocks for student learning and determine next steps for modifying instruction through reteaching, revising strategies, or other instructional interventions. The embedded assessment approach not only enables teachers to "assess to assist," but also offers students clear guidelines for evaluating and monitoring their own learning, and a context for doing so while learning, not just at the end.

Cases in this chapter highlight how ongoing assessment embedded in day-to-day teaching directs next steps, and how teachers use assessments to support students to understand their own learning. Case 8 describes the value of using an array of assessments embedded in the context of balanced literacy instruction. The author argues that these tools provide her with important information about student progress and next steps for

teaching. She also expresses concern that despite changes in her teaching to better support her students, her ongoing assessment data reveal that several children require more assistance than she can offer. In Case 10 on teaching and assessing analytical essay writing, the author describes how her cycle of teaching, assessment, and revision supports students as writers and informs her own practice as a teacher of writing and a designer of rubrics for assessing writing.

Cases 9 and 10 depict how teachers integrate student self-assessment with instruction. In Case 9, a middle grades teacher describes how she promotes student self-assessment of learning—not assessment for grading, accountability, or other purposes, but informal assessment of learning through reflection on what makes a "good reader." She addresses ways to help students be metacognitive about their reading, determining what works well for them and how to improve their ability to comprehend difficult narrative and expository texts. Case 10 describes some of the difficulties teachers confront when using student self-assessment. This author questions what to do with a student who has followed teacher guidelines in a technical sense but who continues to produce writing that does not reach his own expectations.

CASE 8

How Much Is Enough?

Pam Spycher

"This is easy!"

"Watch how I can read this!"

"I'm a good reader now!"

Gina, Peter, and Alexis are reading a simple decodable text from the Scholastic phonics series with me in their skill-based reading group. The book is part of a systematic, explicit phonics reading program and contains decodable CVC words (consonant-vowel-consonant such as cat, mop, tin) with a few high-frequency words sprinkled in. They're reading smoothly and with confidence. They've practiced reading this book several times over the past few days following an initial guided reading lesson that included phonemic awareness, phonics, and spelling practice. We celebrate their success, and the children are eager to move on to the next book in the series.

The next day, after I've reviewed what they've previously learned, introduced the new book, and gone over new vocabulary and word patterns they'll be seeing, the three open their new book and start reading at their own pace.

"This is hard. I don't know if I can read this," Alexis comments.

"Just try your best and tell me if you need help," I suggest.

Meanwhile, Peter is trying his best, but also listening closely to Gina, hoping she can fill in the missing words that he's struggling with. Although not much more difficult than the previous book they learned to read, getting through it was a bit laborious. Gina had an easier time of it, retaining the word patterns and high-frequency words from previous lessons. But Alexis and Pe-

ter struggled, even with some word patterns they had "mastered" a few books before.

It's March of first-grade, and I'm feeling nervous about the rate at which these three are developing in reading. Stanovich (1986) argues that there is strong and persuasive evidence that suggests that children who get off to a slow start in learning decoding skills rarely become strong readers. Gina, Peter, and Alexis are my least proficient readers, growing at a painfully slow rate, and I have doubts that they will even approach the spring first-grade benchmark for reading. They've come a long way, from knowing very few letter sounds and having no phonemic awareness in September, to being able to read simple decodable texts in March. But they are lagging far behind the first-grade exit benchmark, and I'm not very optimistic about them getting up to where their peers will be by the end of first grade. Growth, yes, but where they should be, no. On a developmental reading assessment, they are still at Level 3 (a simple, patterned text with about 30 words, many of them repeated on each page), which was the end of the first quarter fall benchmark for first grade. They need to jump to Level 16 (a text with complicated vowel patterns and over 200 words) by the end of the year. They are struggling, and time is running out.

I've been teaching for three years. Ours is a small school with about 500 students in a district of six elementary schools, two junior highs, and three high schools. There are 18 children of various racial and economic backgrounds in my first-grade class. For the past two years, I've been on our district's Language Arts Task Force and Literacy Assessment committees. Last year, these committees used the California Language Arts Content Standards and other resources to create a district-wide, K–6 standards-based assessment package (see Assessment Processes and Student Data, below). I highly value these assessments, not only because they are aligned with the state standards, but more importantly, because they reflect the most current research on literacy. Therefore, I really do use these assessments to drive my instruction. I feel that, overall, the literacy assessments (especially those that measure phonemic awareness and phonics skills) measure what I am actually teaching, and what I value for students as they develop literacy skills.

Assessment Processes and Student Data

The complex battery of assessments I administer to each student three times a year enables me to pinpoint what my students are ready to learn and when they are ready to learn it. Most of these assessments, required by my school district, were brought to the district by classroom teachers involved in the California Reading and Literature Project's "Results" assessment pilot, and find them extremely valuable for targeting instruction. In first grade, the battery includes three phonemic awareness assessments (blending, segmenting, and rhyming and changing sounds), the BPST (Basic Phonics Skills Test, for phonics and decoding), a reading accuracy assessment, a high-frequency word reading assessment, a developmental spelling assessment, a high-frequency word spelling assessment, and a writing assessment. Although these assessments are extremely time-consuming (most need to be administered individually and take about 10 minutes per student), my colleagues and I feel that they are invaluable. Each assessment looks at literacy in a different way, and each gives a snapshot of what the child can do, what they are using but confusing (this is where instruction is focused), and what is absent in their repertoire. These assessments are not used solely for accountability purposes. They are genuinely used to guide instruction and to communicate with parents the areas in which their children need extra support at school and at home, thereby establishing a purposeful and collaborative relationship between the teacher and the family.

Because these assessments are so important and so time-consuming and because the teacher really does need to administer them to get a true sense of where her students are, our district has provided release time to administer them. The release time is not nearly enough time to administer all of the assessments, but this endeavor would be impossible without at least some release time. There has been an issue of teachers taking on more and more responsibilities without the support to do them effectively. The teachers in our district feel that because these assessments are such an integral part of our instructional program, the district has no choice but to continue to support additional training and provide release time. This truly has been an area where newer and veteran teachers have mutually benefited from each other's expertise and support.

Gina, Peter, and Alexis are not "slow learners," nor are they discipline problems. They are very bright and receptive learners, and Peter, in particular, is one of those kids who would be able to "fake" reading well if I didn't do individual reading assessments. He's a great "shadow reader" and often offers the most insightful input in whole-group literacy activities around comprehension. The three are also angels in terms of behavior. They are incredibly eager and motivated to become stronger, independent readers and always come to reading group enthusiastically. They see that they have not yet made the leaps and bounds in independent reading that their peers have (many of whom are now into chapter books), but this has only made them work harder at practicing books at their reading level in order to get to the next one. All three children love school, are always on time, and rarely miss a day.

Gina and Peter are fraternal twins. They've had a difficult family history. At the beginning of the year, they were homeless, living in a shelter, and their parents recently separated. They actually started the school year four weeks late, as their mother was figuring out their living and family situation. They'd entered our school's kindergarten in midyear of the previous year. Their European mother is not a native English speaker and has had serious health problems related to smoking. Their father is African-American. English is the dominant language spoken in the home, and the children understand a little of their mother's native language. She's changed jobs a few times during the year. She met with me a few times, and I believe that she genuinely wants to help accelerate her children's reading growth, but I'm not sure how much time she can give them in this area. It's easy to tell that these well-behaved children are loved and well cared for by their mother. Gina was a bit shy, especially at the beginning of the year, but both siblings generally exuded self-confidence. However, given their home life, I feel that these children have had fewer literacy opportunities in the home prior to and during first grade.

Alexis is the third and youngest child in an Anglo-American working-class family. His father has gone on almost all of our field trips, and his mother has had frequent contact with me before and after school. At the beginning of the year, Alexis's mother told me she had purchased the Scholastic at-home phonics reading program for her son to help accelerate his reading growth. Unfortunately, I've heard both parents refer to themselves as slow learners, bad readers, or not smart in school, and I've also heard Alexis talk about himself in similar terms (of course, always followed by a long talk with me contradicting these statements). His self-esteem has increased as the year has progressed, and I feel it has something to do with his growth in reading. Alexis had also entered our school's kindergarten program in midyear last year.

As I reflect upon their last text reading and phonics assessment data, I feel the urge to push these three children along at a much quicker pace. They have the lowest scores in the class on these assessments (see Figures 8.1 and 8.2), yet they've received a great deal of individual instruction from me, my aide, and whoever else I've been able to pull in for one-on-one skills practice in phonemic awareness and phonics just to get them to where they are now. My aide or I (or sometimes both, if I had more time) spent 20 to 30 minutes a day with them during the first few months of school, either individually or in pairs, first working on phonemic awareness skills (rhyming, then blending, then segmenting) and letter/sound correspondence, slowly pulling them to a point where they could begin to decode words. In guided reading, I worked with them daily on patterned text until they were ready for decodable text. In addition, our first-grade team asked our school's Title I aide to work with some of our struggling students. She was able to work with Gina and Peter a few days a week for about 15 minutes a day in a group of four to six children (a combined group from all the first-grades) on phonemic awareness for about five weeks. I've spoken with their parents about what particular areas they need to be working on with them at home. I've done what I know how to do best, but could I be doing more to accelerate these struggling readers' growth?

Over the past few years, I've been reflecting a great deal on what my students need to know by the end of first grade, and what activities are most important in order for them to get there. I struc-

FIGURE 8.2. BPST fAssessment Data

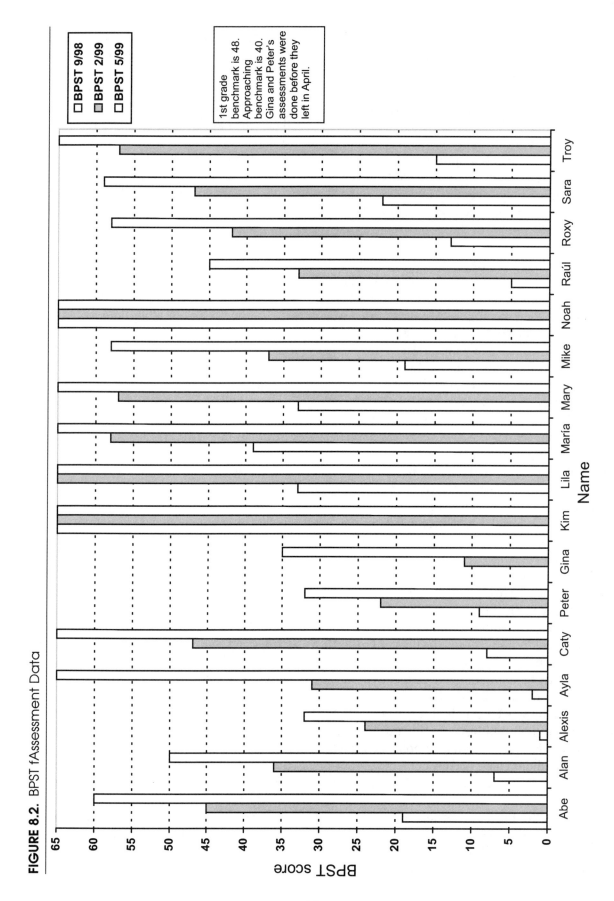

FIGURE 8.3. DRA Assessment Data

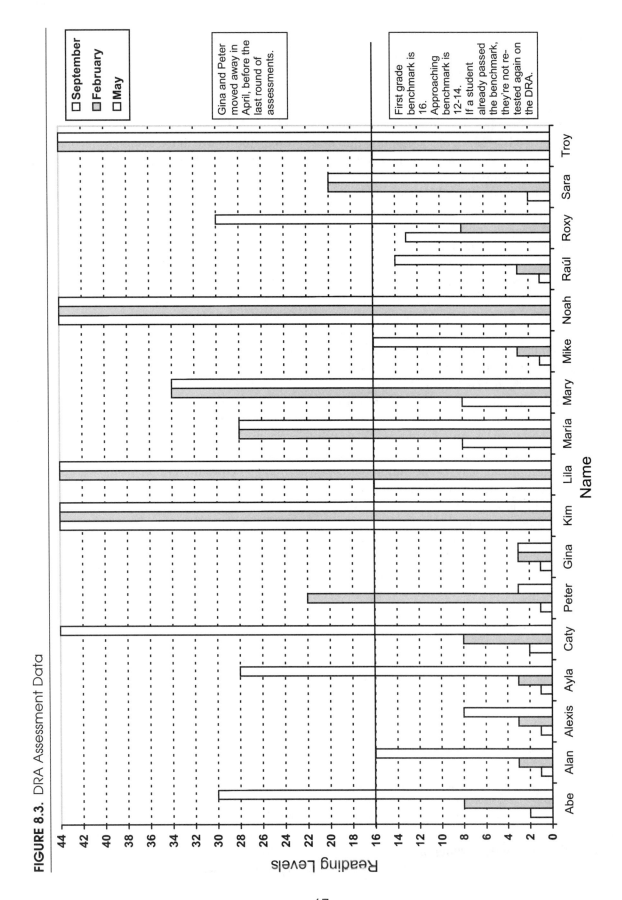

ture the entire morning around literacy. Afternoons are for math, science, and other content areas, with literacy integrated within them. When the children arrive at school, we sing songs that play with language, recite poems we've learned, and play quick phonemic awareness games. Then we begin our reading block of 75 minutes, during which time the students go to open-ended literacy centers where they engage in reading activities (reading books, reading along to a book on tape, constructing poems and sentences at the pocket chart, playing phonics or phonological awareness games). My aide and I pull out students for skill-based reading groups.

For me, this is really the meat of my reading instructional program. This is my time to really use what I've learned from my reading assessments to drive my instruction. I'm able to pull three, sometimes four groups of one to four children daily for reading lessons at their instructional level (based on the assessments) that last from 10 to 25 minutes each. I coordinate with my instructional aide, who pulls small groups as well. This year I've been really lucky, and have had an outstanding student teacher working with groups so that we can pull even more groups each day. Some children are pulled from their centers more than once if they need more help. Some groups are guided reading groups; sometimes what's needed is extra work with phonemic awareness or phonics. We work on reading skills, comprehension, spelling—you name it. I use a variety of instructional materials in my reading program, depending on the needs of the students. I use leveled as well as decodable text. I'm also currently doing literature response groups with chapter books with my higher readers, and some groups have written and performed their own skits based on what they've read in reading groups. Of course, these groups are flexible and constantly shifting, as children move at their own different reading paces.

After recess, we have a 75-minute writing block. We start this time with a shared or interactive writing lesson where we go over spelling patterns, grammar, and other elements of writing. Then we either write in interactive journals or have a Writers' Workshop, where my students go through the steps of the writing process to grow as writers. During this time I work one-on-one

with kids in editing conferences, or pull small, skill-based groups to work on writing skills.

At the end of the day, we go back to reading. Sometimes I'll read aloud, and sometimes a student will read to the class in the "Reader's Chair." Then it's DEAR (Drop Everything And Read) time, during which the students practice reading texts at their instructional level that I have given them at their reading groups in the morning. They usually have about five books at their instructional level, which they must practice reading for fluency before they are able to choose texts from our extensive classroom library. This is my time to assess my students' text reading through running records.

All in all, I devote about 200 minutes to literacy daily, not including the science, math, social studies, and art activities I integrate with literacy in the afternoon. That's a lot of time. This time commitment, combined with my motivation in learning and applying effective literacy strategies, has had a tremendous impact on my practice. My students have all shown enormous growth. Most are incredibly skilled readers and have reached the targeted benchmark three months before the end of first grade. But some kids, like Alexis, Gina, and Peter, continue to lag far behind.

I've spoken with enough upper-grade teachers, who lament that their struggling students are expected to achieve three or four years of reading growth in one school year, to know that first grade is a crucial year in terms of literacy development. In addition, research suggests that if first-graders are not on grade level by the end of the year, chances are they'll be behind their peers for the rest of their schooling (Stanovich, 1986). With a carefully designed, literacy-rich curriculum that is driven by standards-based assessments, and literacy instruction that is tailored to students' needs, why are these students still not even approaching the grade-level benchmark three months before the end of first grade? As I think about promotion to second grade, I wonder if the growth they have made in my classroom—which still falls seriously short of the grade-level exit benchmark—is enough to make them successful learners in the grades to come.

In my first year of teaching, before we began to use standards-based literacy assessments, it was enough for me to see just about any amount of growth. Progress was exciting and made me feel like I was doing my job. But now that I have more detailed information on student growth through the new assessments, I feel that the level of my accountability has been raised. It's exciting and scary at the same time. With the assessments, I feel that I can target the exact needs of each individual student. But what happens when I've done everything I know how to do and they still don't get there? Are children like Gina, Peter, and Alexis doomed to repeat first grade? Is there something that I or the district can do to prevent this?

REFERENCE

Stanovich, K. E. (1986). Matthew effects in reading: Some consequences of individual differences in the acquisition of literacy. *Reading Research Quarterly*, 2, 360–407.

CASE 9

Learning to Read . . . or Reading to Learn

Marlo Chavez

Jeanne, a student in my sixth-grade Language Arts class, struggles with what she reads. She never seems to be at a loss for words during class discussions on reading material, yet the response is usually based on her own experiences and not what she has read. I needed to assess her with our district's reading fluency and comprehension test and was anxious to see the results (see Figure 9.1). During the assessment I had Jeanne read the selected passage, which she read incredibly fast. But she did not use intonation in her voice, she skipped over words, and she added her own words when she felt they were needed, yet she passed the fluency section of the assessment tool. And when I asked, "Jeanne, can you tell me what this story is about?" I looked into her brown eyes and noticed a familiar fear, one that I had felt many times as a student. She could not tell me what she'd read; she hadn't thought about the words as she read them. When she saw the yellow stopwatch in my hand, she had concentrated only on reading fast. Jeanne must think that speed is what makes you a good reader and was now faced with the dilemma of how to think about and understand what she was reading. I felt her pain and wondered how a timed test could effectively assess a student's reading ability.

Our district and state tell us that our students are reading below the state norm in various grade levels. They show as evidence scores from the STAR/SAT 9 standardized test and our district's timed assessments for fluency and comprehension. We are also required to compile our students' writing samples—which we score with rubrics based on the eight Language Arts standards—into portfolios. Teachers use these portfolios as additional evidence of what students learn, but these are rarely part of our accountability profile.

We must be doing something wrong. Most students entering sixth grade cannot read our textbooks, and their test scores are not improving. Our students come primarily from poor and lower-middle-class families, of which a high percentage are single-parent households. Thirty percent of the students use Spanish as their primary language. Considering our population, I could generalize or even justify why our scores are lower than those in other more affluent sections of our state. For the past five years, our students' SAT 9 and district performance assessments have hovered around the 50th percentile in fluency and comprehension. Where is the missing link between what we're teaching and the achievement test results?

I had always assumed that students entering middle school were able to read with understanding. Obviously I have been wrong, as the test scores and my personal observations show. Elementary teachers have access to effective strategies and assessments to help students learn. But we still get students who can decode the words but don't understand what they read. What can we middle school teachers do to help our students?

This year I tried something new in my classroom. My own history as a reader was my impe-

FIGURE 9.1. Comprehension and Fluency Assessment: Teacher Recording Sheet

Name of Child: _____ Date: _____ Grade: ____6____

Action at Brantwood

As Kay got off the passenger train at Brantwood, she was rudely shoved. Turning quickly, she	16
saw a young man elbowing his way through the bustling crowd toward an older woman. As Kay	33
proceeded across the train platform, she saw the older woman trip and tumble to the pavement.	49
The fallen woman's handbag flew open and its contents spilled all over the ground. Her suitcase	65
also snapped open and its contents, too, were strewn over the snow.	7
Kay rushed up to help the stunned woman. She was brushed aside by the man who had collided	95
with her earlier. The man assumed charge of the woman's belongings in a most possessive manner.	111
He was short, slender, blonde, and had a rosy complexion. Kay picked up the woman's handbag	127
from the snow, but the young man snatched it from her almost as if he suspected her of trying to	147
steal it.	149
"Just a minute, please!" exclaimed Kay. "I'm just trying to help this lady. May I ask you why you	167
are trying to take charge of her things?"	175
"I am her son!" retorted the young man unpleasantly as he went on hastily collecting the things	192
which had burst from the suitcase. Kay concentrated her attention on the woman and tried to help	209
her up. "Where are my purse and my suitcase!" she cried anxiously.	221
"Your son has them," Kay said reassuringly. "Don't worry about them. He'll bring you every-	235
thing as soon as he has it all collected."	244
"My son!" the lady exclaimed sharply. "I have no son!"	254

Retell/Comprehension:

4	Excellent
3	Satisfactory, an adequate understanding
2	Some understanding
1	Very little understanding

_____ WPM – Errors = _____

or

_____ WPM – Errors = _____

) 15000

Fluency:

3	Reads fluently with expression, reads the punctuation
2	Reads primarily in phrases, little intonation, ignores some punctuation
1	Primarily word-by-word reading

tus for change and discovery. For much of my life I was able to read the words, yet if you asked me what I had read I could not tell you. In elementary school I was in the red group, the top readers. Being a wannabe teacher in third grade, I was able to read the words with flair and intonation, yet my insides shook with fear at the prospect of being asked what thoughts I had about the reading. As the years progressed, I became the class clown in order to keep my secret. I could not think about the words as I read them; my mind was blank. In high school I learned to get by with excuses and low grades, knowing that attending college was not in my future. As a young adult, I joined an airline and traveled the world to gain an education by experiencing life. It took a jolt in my life, by attending college at 35, to bring my inability to read effectively into my need category. No one had shared with me how to think when you read. I wanted to remember what I'd read and even discuss those issues that I was confused about, but I didn't have a clue about how to achieve this.

While attending college and doing graduate work in education, I was offered many reading methods classes, yet none seemed to address my personal issues and give me answers. But a wonderful thing happened during the past three years. I was able to participate in intensive literacy instruction through the gift of a district grant. We've had many high-powered speakers and time to collaborate and dialogue about our own practice. I became armed with new instructional strategies that needed exploration and fine-tuning, which also helped my own personal journey to understand what it takes to become a good reader. I know that there is no quick cure-all for a middle school student who needs to learn to read and comprehend text. But my own personal and professional journey learning what a good reader does has helped me to articulate this process with my students.

Our discovery began with reading the book *Tuck Everlasting* (Babbitt, 1975). This is one of our sixth-grade core literature books and is full of similes, metaphors, and creative imagery. I asked the class to take the book home and read the prologue and first two chapters. (Reading required literature for homework is a common practice at our site. We use the 43 minutes of class time to do Into, Through, and Beyond strategies and sharing of book reports or creative projects.) The next day, I asked for a show of hands on who would like to describe a scene from what they had read. No one raised his hand. I then asked for the class to take out a piece of paper and draw a scene from one of the pages, and I watched as students hesitated to begin their work. As I walked around the room, I noticed a few students becoming creative, yet their pictures had nothing to do with the reading. One student, when asked, said he was just drawing and didn't know why. It was painful to see students obviously struggling with this assignment. So after waiting an appropriately long enough time for the illustrations to begin, I asked if they wanted to reread the pages together in order to understand what was read. Their response was overwhelmingly unanimous. Many said that the book was hard to understand; all of the students—including the excellent readers—wanted to reread the entire section. My venture in teaching "reading-thinking" had begun!

The first challenge was to help students make connections with their reading. All good readers make three types of connections (from *Mosaic of Thought*, by Ellin Oliver Keene & Susan Zimmermann [1997]):

1. Connect with yourself—something you have experienced.
2. Connect with another book/author—one that reminds you of this one.
3. Connect with the world—possibly something you have seen or read about.

As I orally read from the assigned reading of *Tuck Everlasting*, I intentionally stopped at intervals, making connections and sharing my thoughts.

> This guy reminds me of my friend Rock. He is tall and lanky and wears clothes that look like what this guy is wearing . . . This book reminds me of a book I read when I was a kid about a magical bottle; it was my favorite story because I thought of all sorts of things I could wish for, just by rubbing the bottle! Have you noticed that this author writes with a lot of metaphors? The style of

writing reminds me of an article I read recently about taking the time to think about the pictures you create in your mind's eye while you are reading. When an author uses metaphors, it helps the reader visualize by comparing with a familiar object . . . This section about the hub of a Ferris wheel makes me think about the town in my mind's eye.

I drew a picture of what it looked like to me on the chalkboard. "Is this the picture you see?" Most students responded that they saw a similar picture. When it was time for the students to describe a scene from the book, I was pleased to see that everyone completed the task successfully.

Throughout the first half of the book, I continued to think out loud as I read, periodically stopping to make appropriate connections. Students eventually asked to read and slowly began sharing their connections, until the process of metacognition (i.e., describing, analyzing, and monitoring one's thinking while reading) became a part of our classroom dialogue. I began to incorporate mini-lessons in this process, because a word, concept, or phrase would surface that was not understood. Students became actively involved with their reading and showed dramatic improvement in their dialogue with one another. Reciprocal Teaching[1] took on new directions; more students participated by asking appropriate questions, clarifying information, summarizing, and predicting what came next. Homework assignments and written summaries also improved. I wondered if this was because students had a shared reading experience or because they were more aware of effective reading strategies and could assess their own comprehension.

At the end of reading *Tuck Everlasting*, students shared their thoughts. One said: "This was my favorite book, but if we did not spend time thinking about it, I would never have read this book." Another student responded, "I usually would have looked for an easier book with pictures, because the language was hard. But I liked that we shared our experiences and am glad I didn't change books."

Since this strategy seemed to be working, I wondered if students could transfer our literature-based strategies to the dry content of our social science book. So I decided to attempt something I normally do not do: give a quiz on the reading. During the last half-hour of class, I asked the students to take out their textbook and read pages 186 through 190. "Use whatever strategies work for you that will help you remember what you have read. For those who need it, I have a study guide, which will be placed on the back table. We will have a quiz on the chapter tomorrow." Many students automatically moved into their Reciprocal Teaching groups, and began reading out loud and following the appropriate questioning process. Some picked up the study guide—another of our learning strategies. Others chose to read silently on their own, and a few seemed to be avoiding the reading altogether. The bell rang before the reading was complete (which was planned), and I asked the students to complete the reading at home. They were to come prepared for a short quiz on the material the next day.

As students entered class the next morning, many were obviously stressed. "Can we have an open-book test?" "Can I use my notes?" "Can we have more time to study?" were some of the comments I heard as everyone prepared for the inevitable. The test—titled "How Well Did You Read?"—included six questions, all of which should have been answered effortlessly if students had read the assigned pages. My last instructions, as students began quieting down for the quiz, was for the students to sit quietly as they finished until everyone had completed the quiz. As students began to finish, I noticed many scratching their heads, hoping that a magical cure would enter into their thoughts and the answer would surface. Others seemed to answer the questions effortlessly. When everyone finished, I asked them to turn their papers over and correct their own tests. As the answers were given one by one, we discussed each question. One student described how a museum he went to helped him remember important things. Another noted that the artifacts in ancient Mesopotamia were the same as those in ancient Egypt. Still another student said that he read the same information from another book. I was pleased; connections were definitely happening.

When we finished correcting the test, I asked for a show of hands. "How many of you got all the questions right? Missed one? Two? Three?" I wanted to get a general idea of how many accurately remembered information from the text, and I was disappointed. Although many had made appropriate connections, most had a difficult time remembering the content and failed the quiz. I wondered if making connections with text was only useful with fiction, and wished I knew how to get them to remember information from nonfiction books.

So I tackled my second challenge: How do we think about and remember what we have read? I began by saying, "Whenever I need to remember what I've read, I always need to highlight the area in my book that needs remembering. Since we can't write in our books, what might I do instead?"

"You can use Post-its for the important information," was Dani's response.

I then asked some of the students who had successfully finished the test with little effort if they could share what they did. Michael pointed out that he writes down information. "Sometimes I write certain facts—the ones I think will be important to remember. I usually put them on little cards so I can carry them around and think about them." Leslie said that she writes information on a piece of binder paper, which helps her remember it.

I kept the conversation going by adding a suggestion of my own. "When I want to remember information I've read, I try to share it with someone else. Being a teacher and talking to you about information helps me remember the key points." Then Matt, a strong student who had all six questions right, said that he talked to his mom about the chapter after he had read it twice. "She was really interested and asked a lot of questions which helped me to remember." Another boy said that he had read the chapter out loud to his little brother and then wrote questions a teacher might ask.

By this time, many students had their hands up and began sharing their thoughts. Many had good suggestions, such as, "I think I might like to try making a web like I do in Writer's Workshop; webs help me make pictures in my mind's eye." But others noted that they had problems. "I usually make pictures in my mind," my resident artist said, "but I had a hard time making pictures

from this book." Jason added that he usually has no trouble making connections to help him remember, yet he could not seem to connect with anything from ancient Egypt.

"How about that?" I asked. "Can we help Jason make connections to help him remember?" At this point, many students gave suggestions, which prompted Jason to come up with one of his own. Before we knew it, we had generated a list of strategies to help us remember important ideas:

1. Make connections
2. Read out loud
3. Talk about the reading
4. Write about it—take notes or write summary
5. Highlight important things
6. Reread
7. Make a web
8. Make a picture in your head (movie or snapshot)
9. Ask questions to yourself and others
10. Become an actor in the reading[2]

This list is posted in our room. Students also have a copy for their binders.

After I began to use these strategies, I thought that students showed some improvement in their reading and motivation to learn. But I was disappointed to learn, at the end of the year, that their improvement had not shown up on their SAT 9 test and only marginally on the district fluency assessment. The majority of students still remained at the 50th percentile. I wondered what was being assessed by the SAT 9 and how it related to the strategies I was teaching. Why didn't these strategies transfer to the testing context of the SAT 9? Jeanne was an exception; her comprehension score rose dramatically. I wondered why. Was it because we explored ways to see beyond the written word? Was it because she was one of the few students who actively engaged in the required reading for 20 minutes per day at home?

My colleagues and I are still looking for ways to help our students improve their reading skills. As I look ahead to next year, I'm prone to continue focusing on the thinking process during reading because I believe it's an essential part of becoming a good reader. But even if my students get better at it, will it show up in their test scores?

Aren't there other assessments that can give us more guidance with our instruction?

NOTES

1. Reciprocal Teaching (RT) was designed by Ann Marie Palincsar and Ann Brown in 1984. RT provides students with a set of cognitive strategies that enable the reader to have greater access and understanding of the text. Through a variety of questions first modeled by an adult, the child learns the importance of clarifying, predicting, summarizing, and interpreting newly revealed material. After seeing strategies modeled by an adult, students are encouraged to take turns being the "teacher." Eventually all RT groups are directed by the students themselves. For more information on Reciprocal Teaching, see Figure 14.1 in Case 14 of this volume.

2. These strategies are based on the theory that if we understand what goes on in the mind of a good reader, we can think those thoughts ourselves and our reading will improve. They are adapted from *Mosaic of Thought*, by Ellin Oliver Keene and Susan Zimmermann (1997).

REFERENCES

Babbitt, N. (1975). *Tuck everlasting*. New York: Farrar, Straus, Giroux.

Keane, E. O., & Zimmermann, S. (1997). *Mosaic of thought*. Portsmouth, NH: Heinemann.

CASE 10

Using Rubrics to Teach Analytic Essay Writing

Kerrin Murphy

"But you have to use evidence from the text to support your ideas and your ideas have to support your opinion. This is what you need to know how to do when you get to middle school!" I was telling this to Esteban, one of my fifth-grade students, during a revision conference, going over first drafts of an analytical essay.

Esteban looked at me, a bit perplexed. He then said, "But isn't this what you wanted me to do, teacher?" I looked at his perfectly formed introductory paragraph, a virtual photocopy of the example I had given my students when teaching them how to write an introductory paragraph. The only difference was that he had plugged in his own information. When I wrote, "I believe the family in the book *The Animal Family* [Jarrell, 1996] is a real family because I think that families show love for each other," in his essay he wrote, "I believe that the family in the book *The Animal Family* is not a real family because I think that families have to be related to each other."

At that moment, my proverbial lightbulb went on. What Esteban gets, I realized, is that the teacher wants him to do this, but he doesn't know how or why. He wants to make me happy and he's copying my example and plugging in his own information, but that's not going to make him a better essay writer.

My goal was for all of my students to become independent essay writers. I had designed some mini-lessons about how to write a persuasive five-paragraph essay and even gave them a model. But my assessment of their first essays showed me that not only Esteban but also several other students used my model too literally. What was I to do? I knew that I'd have to revise my strategies of teaching expository writing to enable the students to become more independent. I was also anxious about middle school the following year and had wanted to protect them from its sink-or-swim nature. But perhaps I should be honest and say something like, "You need to know this, because next year you will be evaluated, judged, and possibly tracked according to whether you are successful or not."

I'm a bilingual teacher who teaches a fourth and fifth grade combination at a professional development school in a rural community in California. My students stay with me for two years, beginning in fourth grade. Our school has a predominantly Latino population, many of whom are in migrant education. Most students get financial support for lunch. During the three years I've been teaching at this site, I've worked closely with my grade-level team. We plan most of our units together. I also collaborate with several different organizations and mentors to increase my effectiveness as a beginning classroom instructor.

During the last few years, we have been working on using a model of multicultural education developed by James Banks, in which we look at academic content critically as teachers and as students (Banks & Banks, 1995). We find, develop, and use resources that reflect the cultural heritage of the students we teach as well as those we don't teach. We have also been working on understanding the value and application of authentic assessment. This means developing ways to assess where students are in their academic knowledge, and using the assessments to guide our instruction to raise their performance to the next level. My dilemma on teaching persuasive essay writing is a case in point.

Our first whole-class book, *The Animal Family* by Randall Jarrell (1996), explored the themes of who we are and who our families are. I thought that reading this book would be an excellent way of getting to know each other as well as developing a broader definition of "family" by examining alternative family arrangements. The book is a beautiful, poetic story about how a lonely hunter finds happiness with his extended, unusual family—a mermaid, a bear, a lynx, and a young orphaned boy. The themes are broad but mainly focus on family unity: acceptance of and adaptation to life changes, supporting loved ones, happiness from interactions, not possessions, and the biggest theme—alternative family arrangements.

We used a literature method to study this book. The process begins with reading a designated part of a book, no more. Then students write a response to the section that they read using sentence starters that promote analytical thinking. When they are done, they do a vocabulary-building exercise and then get ready to go to their discussion group. While the students are doing this, I meet with a discussion group about what they read and wrote the day before. In this way, I can meet with two or three groups per day. This is where the deep and rich literature analysis is explored and also where students practice forming and building on their and others' opinions and perspectives. It is also a way for students to develop cognitively and apply this in their expository writing skills.

After the class has completed a book, one of the ways we tie it all together and further explore their discussion ideas is to write an analytical essay on a stated opinion and to support that opinion with their ideas and evidence from the book. Since knowing how to write an analytical essay is a fundamental academic skill and since about 80% of the writing we do as adults is nonfiction, I have made this type of writing—defending your opinion with evidence from a text—the foundation of my writing instruction.[1] I realized that the main thread linking our discussion groups on *The Animal Family* was an ongoing debate about whether this could be a "real" family or not. Some students thought that it was, since there is love, respect, and caring. Other students questioned how a real family could have a mermaid, a bear, a lynx, and an adopted little orphaned boy. In other words, with no mother, father, and child, it's not a "traditional" family. I decided to make this the foundation question for their analytical essay: Is this group of creatures a real family? Why or why not?

I broke down the skills I wanted them to develop and taught mini-lessons on the five-paragraph essay. They consisted of introductory and concluding paragraphs with topic sentences and a summary of their opinion and ideas included in each; and the main three-paragraph body, with each paragraph focused on one idea that supported the opinion and each idea supported by a piece of evidence from the text. The students used the writing process of prewriting, first draft, sharing and revision, editing, and final draft.

I modeled each step of the mini-lessons. For example, I showed them this model of an introductory paragraph:

> I believe that the family in the book *The Animal Family* is a real family. I think this because in families the members love each other. They also support each other when they need it. Finally, they protect each other. This is why it is apparent that the hunter, the mermaid, the bear, the lynx and the little boy are a family.

After the essays were written, I made a rubric of skills to assess their and my performance in this first analytical essay for all of us. This rubric was based on all of the mini-lessons I had taught (see Figures 10.1a/b, 10.2a/b, 10.3a/b). I had my students self-assess using the same rubric and then I assessed them.

I had expected the students to have an introductory paragraph that stated their opinion, and then to support it with concrete evidence from the text. For example, in their introductory paragraphs, I wanted them to state their opinion about

FIGURE 10.1A. Analytical Essay Rubric, Student #1

Name/*Nombre*: _____	1) Beginning *Empezando*	2) OK *Más o menos*	3) Good *Bién*	4) Excellent *Excelente*
1. Word web *Cadena de palabras*			√	
2. Idea and evidence page *Hoja de ideas y evidencia*		√		
3. Introductory paragraph *Párrafo de introducción*			√	
** states opinion *dice la opinión*			√	
** states 3 ideas *dice las 3 ideas*		√		
4. 3 paragraphs *3 párrafos*			√	
** states ideas *dice las ideas*			√	
** uses evidence to support ideas *usa evidencia para apoyar las ideas*		√		
5. Concluding paragraph *Párrafo de conclusión*			√	
** states opinion *dice la opinión*			√	
** summarizes ideas *resume las ideas*			√	
6. Does the essay support the opinion? *¿La obra apoya la opinión?*		8 √	24	
Total			32	

A+	A	A-	B+	B	B-	C+	(C)	C-	D+	D	D-	F	**Grade/**
48	46	44	42	40	37	35	33	30	27	24	21	20	***Calificación:*** *C*

Comments/*Commentarios*:

Good job, but I would like you to remember to use evidence from the book.

FIGURE 10.1B. Student #1 Essay

I don't think they are a real family in the book <u>Animal Factory</u>. I now that they help eachother and that staff but I think that they are just friends and live together. They came from diffrent places.

I think in the book <u>Animal Factory</u> that they are not a real family. It is becose they came from diffrent places and the story may be old. When they were they were there it may have been elagle to have a diffrent family.

I think that hunter could go to jail if there was a police becose the hunter stoled the Lynx and the bear and found the boy. And they did think that if they found a boy or a girl they would have to have it turned it in some where.

I think that they are diffrent and they are a family there could be trouble. Becose they do things diffrently and my be they want everyone to do this but evreyone wants to do it there way and they can get into a fight.

I conclusion, I don't think that they are a real family becose they come from diffrent places and they even stole some of the (unreadable text). The ather things is if they want to do something and the other person wants to do something then evreyone will fight and get mad. I dont want to be in this family.

---

the family, and then describe three ideas that supported their opinion. The following is a good example of what I wanted:

> It is clear that when reading the book *The Animal Family* the hunter, the mermaid, the bear, the lynx and the little boy make up a loving family. In families there is love, families support each other and family members protect each other.

Overall, they did a good job. However, I was disappointed to see that what they produced was cookie cutter and obviously based on my model. Here is a typical example:

> I believe that the family in the book *The Animal Family* is a real family. I think this because families respect each other. They also care for each other when they need it. Finally, they defend each other. This is why it is apparent that the hunter, the mermaid, the bear, the lynx and the little boy are a family.

My dilemma was that I wasn't really sure if I was scaffolding them appropriately to promote independent analytical essay writing or if I was

missing the mark entirely. The conversation with Esteban tended to support my doubts. I also questioned whether they could become independent writers at this point of their development. But with the middle school clock ticking louder, I was nervous about its unsupportive environment and felt I should push ahead.

As I planned the next unit, I realized that they had indeed accomplished what I had asked of them. They had already written a five-paragraph essay, complete with an introduction, a body, and a conclusion. And they had also formed an opinion, developed ideas to support their opinion, and supported their ideas with evidence from the text. I wanted to enhance the skills they had begun acquiring, and wondered how I could further develop my instruction and their production. How can I withdraw scaffolds to promote independence? And how do I cram all of this in before they leave me in June?

My solution was to revise my instruction for the second analytical essay by providing a more flexible structure, since they had had a fairly rigid one to begin with. The challenge was to strike a perfect balance between scaffolding and independence.

This time we were studying discrimination—in ourselves, on television, and in society. My stu-

FIGURE 10.2A. Analytical Essay Rubric, Student #2

Name/*Nombre*: _____	1) Beginning *Empezando*	2) OK *Más o menos*	3) Good *Bién*	4) Excellent *Excelente*
1. Word web *Cadena de palabras*				√
2. Idea and evidence page *Hoja de ideas y evidencia*				√
3. Introductory paragraph *Párrafo de introducción*			√	
** states opinion *dice la opinión*		√		
** states 3 ideas *dice las 3 ideas*		√		
4. 3 paragraphs *3 párrafos*			√	
** states ideas *dice las ideas*			√	
** uses evidence to support ideas *usa evidencia para apoyar las ideas*		√		
5. Concluding paragraph *Párrafo de conclusión*				√
** states opinion *dice la opinión*				√
** summarizes ideas *resume las ideas*			√	
6. Does the essay support the opinion? *¿La obra apoya la opinión?*		6	15 √	16
Total		37		

A+	A	A-	B+	B	B-	C+	C	C-	D+	D	D-	F	**Grade/ Calificación:**
48	46	44	42	40	37	35	33	30	27	24	21	20	*B-*

(B- is circled)

Comments/Commentarios:

You have improved your essay writing skills a lot! What is missing is the background information about the book. What if the reader has never read "Molly's Pilgrim" before? Also, make sure you use "facts" that you know are true. In your conclusion you say that discrimination is killing too many people but Molly didn't die and that's a big statement.

FIGURE 10.2B. Student #2 Essay

<u>Introduction</u>

I think that it isin't fear that Molly gets discrimanated against a lot just because she does mastakes in English and she talk's funny. Because they always watting to see that Molly does a mastake to laugh at her. I think it heart a lot her feelings and it isin't fear.

I think that Elizabeth was not helping. She didin't want to help her and insted she did warse problems for Molly. Like when she Molly was reading a book she didn't now a word and Elizabeth said that she will be a Tanksgiving. And she said that evreone nows that. Not evreone nows that.

Elizabeth was alway's discrimanated at Molly. But too Elizabeth thought that she was funny. But I said no. Because you are hearting feelings to someone.

Elizabeth laugh and heated the culture of Molly she hated so much that she could killed Molly. I got the feeling that Elizabeth think's that her culture is the best. I think that all the cultures are good and I like it.

<u>Conclusion</u>

I think that discrimanation is killing too many people and is because they are mybe not a good people. But people are prejuding against evreone. That is what heart Molly too much. But too Molly could it beat discrimanation and there is nothing to be afriad.

dents had just finished reading a literature array about prejudice and resilience when I launched the new unit. I followed the literature circles format with the exception that groups of four to six students read different books on more or less the same theme. We also developed a matrix of information for students to experience what the rest of the groups were reading. This matrix was also used as a scaffold for the essay writing to come.

But instead of going directly into directions for writing an essay like we did during the first unit, I passed out the rubric and used it as a guide. I showed them exactly how I would assess their work, sharing my expectations and grading process.

The question for this essay was very general: What has this book taught you about prejudice and discrimination? As a whole class, we reviewed the content of the rubric: What's included in an introductory paragraph? What is evidence from the text? And so forth. The following typifies the kind of introductory paragraph I looked for:

The book *Amazing Grace* [1991] taught me that there are several different kinds of discrimination. In this book there was

sexism and racism. I think that discrimination hurts all the participants in many ways. It hurt Grace because she was hurt by discriminatory comments by thinking that she couldn't be Peter Pan in the play because she was an African-American. It hurt the boy who discriminated against her because he was showing his ignorance. . . .

We discussed in detail the grading system based on the rubric. To get a 0, there would have to be no introductory paragraph. To get a 1, they stated their opinion and developed rudimentary ideas to support it. To get a 2, they stated their opinion and developed good ideas to support it. To get a 3, they stated their opinion and developed very good ideas to support it. To get a 4, they stated their opinion and developed excellent ideas to support it. I also showed specific examples from students' work on the first analytical essay (without using their names), which was my revised approach of modeling. My students couldn't possibly copy anything, since they would be working on a completely different theme.

Then I said, "GO!" And with very little support—just the matrix, the rubric, and a series of

FIGURE 10.3A. Analytical Essay Rubric, Student #3

Name/*Nombre*: _____	1) Beginning *Empezando*	2) OK *Más o menos*	3) Good *Bién*	4) Excellent *Excelente*
1. Word web *Cadena de palabras*				√
2. Idea and evidence page *Hoja de ideas y evidencia*				√
3. Introductory paragraph *Párrafo de introducción*				√
** states opinion *dice la opinión*				√
** states 3 ideas *dice las 3 ideas*				√
4. 3 paragraphs *3 párrafos*				√
** states ideas *dice las ideas*				√
** uses evidence to support ideas *usa evidencia para apoyar las ideas*				√
5. Concluding paragraph *Párrafo de conclusión*				√
** states opinion *dice la opinión*				√
** summarizes ideas *resume las ideas*				√
6. Does the essay support the opinion? *¿La obra apoya la opinión?*				√

Total	*48*

A+	A	A-	B+	B	B-	C+	C	C-	D+	D	D-	F
48	46	44	42	40	37	35	33	30	27	24	21	20

(A+ circled)

Grade/Calificación: *A+*

Comments/Commentarios:

Excellent Job! You really know how to use evidence from the text to support your ideas.

FIGURE 10.3B. Student #3 Essay

<u>Introduction</u>

This book taught me I should be more brave and I should stand up for my self. Aekyung was discriminated because the kid's thought she was chinese. Aekyung was also discriminated because she had korean eye's. The kid's thought the were chinese eye's so they teased her. Aekyung felt bad because people laughed and hurt her feeling's. Aekyung's Dream has thing's you could do to help to make friend's. If you don't know English learn and mabey you'll feel better. Aekyung felt better when she learned english.

<u>3 Paragraphs</u>

My 1st idea is when Aekyung was called hey chinese. She felt very bad and she don't wan't to go to school the next day but she did. My evedince is that Aekyung was called hey chinese. She was discriminated of who she was. She told the kid's she was Korean. Aekyung learnd more english and made new friend's.

My second idea is Aekyung was called chinese eye's. My evidence is that Aekyung said in her head "doesn't any body know about Koreans!" She was mad. One day Aekyung painted a picture.

My third idea is Aekyung was brave and she finally standed up for herself. My evedindince is that Aekyung drew a picture of king sejong. Aekyung had people all around her. There was one boy that teased her. He said "your a good Korean painter". In her amagination king sejong helped her.

<u>Conclusion</u>

My conclusion is Aekyung was called hey chinese. She didn't I like it. She said "I'am Korean"! She was also discriminated because the kid's thought she had chinese eye's. Then she standed up for herself. I was discriminated once because I had a long braid. I didn't like to be teased. A boy teased me then one day the boy stopped. I didn't like to be discriminated. I won't be discriminated any more because I will stand up for myself.

---

review lessons—I asked them to show me what they could do, and show me they did. When we finished, I asked them to self-assess using the rubric and to get a peer assessment using the rubric, and then I assessed them using the rubric.

When I finally read their work I was very surprised. The students surpassed my expectations and had accomplished what I wanted them to with a deeper understanding about how to do it. This was Esteban's introductory paragraph from his second analytical essay:

In the book *Cheyenne Again* [1995], I think it's discrimination when people are forced to give up their cultures. I think it's sad that Cheyenne children were taken from their homes and put into boarding schools.

Forcing someone to not speak their language is discrimination. Making a person from another culture dress like their culture is discrimination. I think it's sad that Americans did these things to Native Americans. This is discrimination.

I was pleased to see much more independently developed ideas and an ability to use evidence from the text accurately to support their ideas. In comparing their first attempt and their second, I wondered if by showing them each step I held them back. Or maybe they needed the highly scaffolded approach the first time to be successful with a more unstructured approach the next time.

At this point, my students were still very far from being independent essay writers. Though proud of my students for their accomplishments, I am still unsatisfied and have many questions: How can I enable them to deepen and solidify their work? How do I start to focus on the detail and variety of analytical essay writing? How can I make peer assessment and self-assessment less token and more authentic? How can I truly promote independence but still scaffold and assist adequately, given that my students come to my class at different levels of development? And finally, how do I assess independence?

NOTE

1. I also incorporate the Writer's Workshop process, developed by Lucy Calkins (1986) and Nancy Atwell (1987), for the development of creative and fictional writing, journal writing for the development of writing for expression, and writing about science and math for the development of writing about other content areas.

REFERENCES

Atwell, N. (1987). *In the middles: Writing, reading, and learning with adolescents.* Portsmouth, NH: Heinemann.

Banks, J. A., & Banks, C. M. (Eds.). (1995). *Handbook of research on multicultural education.* New York: Macmillan.

Bunting, E. (1995). *Cheyenne again* (I. Toddy, Illustrator). New York: Clarion Books.

Calkins, L. M. (1986). *The art of teaching writing.* Portsmouth, NH: Heinemann.

Hoffman, M. (1991). *Amazing grace* (C. Binch, Illustrator). New York: Dial Books for Young Readers.

Jarrell, R. (1996). *The animal family.* (M. Sendak, Illustrator). New York: HarperCollins Juvenile Books.

CHAPTER 4

Using Assessments as Tools for Reporting and Grading

In the past few years, increased attention has been paid to the use of student portfolios and rubrics for formative and summative assessment purposes. In the best of all possible worlds, these portfolios contain samples of the students' best work, assessed with thoughtful rubrics, developmental scales, or other criterion-referenced tools that exemplify specific skills represented at different levels. The benefits of these portfolios are numerous. Students have an active role in selecting work and reflecting on their progress, and teachers have a rigorous and relevant communication vehicle for reporting student progress to parents.

However, dilemmas may arise when teachers—especially those who are novices with this approach—neglect to think through, in advance, what kinds of assignments are most appropriate for the portfolios and how to systematically evaluate the contents of the portfolios. When grading periods arrive and teachers are required to report student progress to parents, these teachers struggle to find meaningful and efficient ways to use the portfolios in their evaluations. Their problems are compounded when teachers ignore the importance of developing a shared understanding with their students about how their work will be evaluated and reported to parents.

A similar situation happened to the author of Case 12. Her dilemma was magnified by the requirement of creating narrative evaluations for her students' report cards. This case raises issues that range from developing appropriate assessment systems and using them as tools for reporting and grading, to enlisting participation of students to assess themselves.

Another challenge to using assessments as tools for reporting and grading concerns rubrics. Teachers often spend hours developing their rubrics, as some cases in this volume illustrate (see Cases 5, 6, 7, and 10). But sometimes they don't understand the limitations of the rubrics until they are sufficiently field-tested with students. This is what happened to the teacher in Case 11, who finds herself in a dilemma when several students' papers meet the highest criteria on a rubric but do not meet her own ideas of top-quality work.

Finding the Right Words

Jean Babb

"I hate words," pouted Larry, the math genius. "They have too many meanings."

Words are my stock in trade as an English Language Arts teacher, so Larry's words concerned me. Larry, his mother, and I were in the midst of a conference about a paper I had just returned to him. His mother wanted to know why he had not been awarded a 6 on his paper. It was a good question, since his paper had met the given criteria for a 6.

I teach seventh-grade English Language Arts in a middle school in Silicon Valley. Our classrooms are heterogeneously grouped, and our school houses the middle school programs for the non-English proficient students and most of the special education students. The English Language Arts teachers at my middle school have agreed to use the writing materials that had been developed at the state level years ago to teach the domains of writing across the three grades, 6 to 8. These state writing materials from the California Assessment Program (CAP) and the California Learning Assessment System (CLAS) tie into my district's expected student learning results for the middle school, support the California English Language Arts Framework, and meet proposed national and state standards.

I am comfortable with the CAP/CLAS materials because I read papers for the state for three years, and as part of the training for the reading, we discussed selected papers, defining the differences between a 5 paper and a 6 paper, how to tell the difference between a "high" 4 and a "low" 5, and

how language conventions fit into the score. Each reader tackled hundreds of papers from across the state. Because I could see the effectiveness of using the materials to holistically score papers, I have been using the CAP/CLAS materials for six years with my own classes. Students are always given the rubric before we begin writing, and we use the writing process (brainstorming, prewriting, first draft, peer editing, proofreading, second draft, conferencing, final draft, publishing).

In order to cover all eight of the CAP/CLAS domains across three years, the English Language Arts teachers divide up the writing work, assigning the domains of autobiographical incident, story, and report of information to the sixth-grade. The seventh-grade teachers "review" those domains and teach observation, evaluation, firsthand biography, and autobiographical incident. The eighth grade teachers review everything and teach the domains of problem/solution and speculation about causes and effects. Students store a paper representing each domain in their student writing portfolios, and the papers accumulate over the three years the students spend at our school. In addition, the autobiographical incident is written each year as a benchmark paper, whereby parents, students, and teachers can see growth in writing ability over time. Because we know that students write what they know best, we feel that the autobiographical incident allows each student to do her or his best.

Larry's mother still sat in front of me, waiting for an answer.

Throughout the year, I taught the students the writing process, and we had already used the CAP/CLAS rubrics for an observation paper and the firsthand biography paper. This year, I had come to the spot in the curriculum where I like to have the students write their autobiographical incidents. I always enjoy these papers because I learn so much about my students.

The autobiographical incident rubric is dense. The criteria for a 6 paper reads:

The student:
- produces a coherent, dramatically realized narrative that relies on a variety of appropriate strategies
- successfully orients readers by presenting context, scene, and people
- states or implies significance of the incident

Years ago, I translated all of the rubrics into more "kid-friendly" language and used the power of the computer to highlight words and phrases that the students might pay special attention to (see Figure 11.1). I always go over the rubric, explaining the tough terms. This year we read through a couple of examples, looking for evidence of the criteria for a 6 paper. We talked about plot and unity and coherence and figurative language.

In the next step, each student created a brainstorm, in the form of a timeline, picking out five important things that had happened to him or her since the end of fifth grade. We went back over the rubric, each student selected an incident that she or he felt would satisfy the rubric, and we were off on the first draft. We worked through the writing process: first draft, peer review, proofreading, second draft, conference/teacher edit, final draft.

At last it was time for me to score the papers holistically. Most of the errors had been caught during the writing process, and during conference/teacher edit, I had made comments and suggestions to students on what to improve to move toward a 6. I turned off the TV, got a Diet Pepsi, put up my feet, and started to read.

I was in trouble. To my surprise, several papers met all of the stated criteria for a 6, but they were not "truly" 6 papers. They were mechanical.

They used uninteresting words and added dialogue for the sake of adding dialogue. And those papers closely mimicked the model I had given them. Larry was the writer of such a paper.

Larry's paper, which had met all of the criteria for a 6 on the rubric, had been scored as a 5. Mrs. L. pointed out that English was Larry's hardest subject, and he had really worked hard to get a 6, so that he would have all As on his report card.

To myself I thought, "What is an A? Is it just meeting criteria? Or does it require something more? What is the grade for meeting the criteria, then? Are A students truly equally excellent in all subjects? Is my A the equivalent of Mr. Hills's A?"

Mrs. L. continued, "You said to use dialogue; there is dialogue. You said it had to have similes and metaphors. Larry had one of each. You said the paper should have a plot; it did. Why is this paper not a 6?"

Then his mother asked another question that I had been wrestling with: How would this grade be incorporated into the overall grade for the quarter? The autobiographical incident had been a major assignment. We had spent five class periods, plus parts of other periods, over three weeks completing the assignment. "What is the grade equivalent of a 5, or a 6, anyway?" she demanded.

"I hate words," pouted Larry, the math genius. "They have too many meanings."

And to myself I mused, "And what about numbers? Is using standard deviations from a mean any more meaningful than using a rubric? Do numbers help a student know what to do to improve performance? Do percentiles and quartiles demonstrate ability any more clearly than rubric scores?"

My experience over the past eight years had taught me that Larry's paper did not deserve a 6, but the paper met the criteria (see Figure 11.2). What words could I use to explain to Larry and his mother that there was more to a 6 than meeting the criteria that were originally stated? How could I explain that Larry's paper lacked "quality?" How could I explain to them what Larry needed to do to have me pencil that 6 onto his paper?

Finally, I explained to Mrs. L. that a "true 6" is a very rare thing (see Figure 11.3 for sample of a "6"), and that a 5 was "above average." Certainly Larry had nothing to worry about as far as his grade because this was one grade among many for the quarter. Larry and his mom finally left. None of us felt very good about what had happened.

Wearily, I collected my mail from the office. There was a message from Mr. G., who wanted to discuss his daughter's score on her autobiographical incident. And there was a note from my principal, who wanted to discuss rubrics.

FIGURE 11.1. Autobiographical Incident: The Rubric (Criteria) and An Exemplary Essay: "Unexpected Friends"

Babb   **Name** _____

English   **Period** _____

Autobiographical Incident
The Rubric (Criteria)

The Autobiographical Incident invites you to tell a story from your personal experience and tell readers what it has meant to you. The best writers orient readers to the incident, present the scene and other people who were present, and then tell an engaging story which may include dialogue, movement or gestures, names of people or objects, and sensory details. You would describe your remembered feelings, understandings, or reflections at the time of the incident and evaluate the incident from your present perspective.

6: Exceptional Achievement (Reader reaction: WOW! Goosebumps. Tears.)
The student
- produces a *coherent*, dramatically realized <u>narrative</u> that relies on a variety of appropriate strategies **successfully orients** readers by presenting <u>context, scene, and people</u>
- STATES OR IMPLIES SIGNIFICANCE OF THE INCIDENT

5: Commendable achievement (Reader reaction: Good story.)
The student
- produces a *coherent*, engaging <u>narrative</u> that **successfully orients** readers
- lacks insight and range of strategies of the writer of a 6 essay
- STATES OR IMPLIES SIGNIFICANCE OF THE INCIDENT

4: Adequate Achievement (Reader reaction: Good try. Got it.)
The student
- produces a well-told <u>incident</u> but lacks the momentum and interest of a 5 or 6 essay
- **orients** readers adequately
- STATES OR IMPLIES SIGNIFICANCE but usually adds it to the end of the narrative

3: Some Evidence of Achievement (Reader reaction: O.K.)
The student
- produces a <u>narrative</u> that is either brief or rambling
- includes only a limited STATEMENT OR IMPLICATION OF SIGNIFICANCE

2: Limited Evidence of Achievement (Reader reaction: Try again.)
The student
- produces general or fragmentary <u>narrative</u>
- includes little if any **orientation** or reflection on SIGNIFICANCE

1: Minimal Evidence of Achievement (Reader reaction: Too bad.)
The student
- responds to prompt but with only the hint of a <u>narrative</u>

FIGURE 11.1. (*continued*)

IN OTHER WORDS, for a paper that demonstrates <u>exceptional achievement</u> (a 6), you must think about and use the following ideas. Papers that do less than this are not a 6.

___Is your paper coherent? A coherent paper is only about **one** thing.
  – Is it all about one incident? (If it is a series of incidents strung together, as in a trip, pick the <u>key</u> incident to write about. Think about why the trip was worth your time to write, the time in the trip that you learned the most, the thing that happened that meant the most to you.)
  – Have you spent time showing the incident?
  – Does the story move toward a central, defining moment (an aha!, a climax, a "knock on the side of the head")?

___Does your paper contain some of the following things?
  – names: specific names of people or objects (names may be changed to protect the innocent), quantities, numbers;
  – visual details of the scene, objects, or people (size, colors, shapes, features, dress);
  – sounds or smells of the scene;
  – specific narrative action (movements, gestures, postures, expressions);
  – dialogue;
  – interior monologue;
  – expression of remembered feelings or insights at the time of the incident;
  – suspense or tension;
  – surprise;
  – comparison or contrast to other scenes or people.

___Have you provided the reader with a context?
  Have you located the incident in a particular setting, introducing the reader to the scene, the people, and the events? Have you carefully chosen details relevant to the incident? Will the reader know why he/she is here? Do you have a balance between description and action?

___Have you revealed why the incident was important to you? The significance may be stated or implied, stated in your insights at the time of the incident or in reflections from your current perspectives, woven through or part of a well-crafted conclusion, may be humorous.

___Does the reader hear your voice as it reveals your attitude towards the incident?

___Does your paper have style?
  – well-chosen details;
  – well-chosen words;
  – graceful, varied sentences;
  – word play and imagery.

FIGURE 11.1 (*continued*)

An Exemplary Essay: "Unexpected Friends"

"Open your books to page 67, please," Mrs. Taylor announced.

"Oh no," I thought. "Why can't you just let us out for our snack break a few minutes early? There are only three minutes left!"

"Now you may go to get your snack," Mrs. Taylor finally said. These were the words I was waiting to hear. As Tina, my best friend, and I jogged down the hall to the principal's office, the banging of lockers and swarm of students were a blur to my eyes and ears. What are the results? What are the results? These four simple words kept racing through my head as I focused my eyes on the long hallway ahead. It was only last Friday, the day of the student council elections, that my friend Mary and I had competed for president and vice-president against two other teams. There had been a tie between us and one of our opponents, a boys' team of Mark and Hal. Now, only two hours ago the final runoff took place. What are the results? I slowed my jog down to a trot, trying to stay calm. There was Mr. Corey's office in front of me—a bear's den, big and foreboding. "Tina, I can't go through with this."

"I'll ask him," she replied decisively as she bounded into his office.

"Who won?"

He paused a moment, taking his hands out of his pockets. His eyes looked past me as he simply stated, "The boys."

Before I knew it, we were back in the hall, heading for the bathroom. Just as we were almost to our destination, just steps away, guess who we had to bump into—Mark, Hal, and Andy, their campaign manager. Andy bellowed, "Who won?" Although I had the fakest smile ever plastered on my face, they did not get the clue.

"You did, and congratulations," I answered in a high squeaky voice.

As I walked back into the classroom, eyes downcast, Mr. Corey's voice came on the loud speaker. "Congratulations to Mark and Hal, our new president and vice-president." Everyone in my class turned to look at me.

My lips, although barely visible, were trembling as I sat down in my seat staring at the desk top. I pushed my hair in front of my face hoping to conceal my flushed cheeks and my sweaty forehead. Why did they have to watch me? I got up to get a drink. AT least that was my excuse, but I wanted to hide the tear that was trickling down my face. On my way to the fountain, Steve came over to me.

"I thought you gave the best speech at the assembly last week, and I think you would have made a good president, too." I looked up at him in disbelief.

"Thanks," I mumbled with a slight smile. As I was bending over to get my drink, Ed came up to me.

"Are you okay? Do you need some help?"

"I'm all right," I replied, but now a bigger smile spread over my whole face. "I didn't need to cry over this," I thought and sat back down at my desk. "Mark and Hal are going to be a very qualified team. Now I don't have to plan out and attend student council meetings." But as much as I tried to convince myself that I didn't care, I was only half listening. Yet that was the first time I realized that sometimes in the time of deepest need, unexpected friends can cheer you up the most.

FIGURE 11.2. Larry's Paper

It was interesting going back to my old school over Christmas. My cousin and I were tired of playing chess, so we sauntered over to my old elementary school. We glided up the path to the office. The red rose trees seemed smaller. At the office, we turned right, and when we got to the end of the building, we turned left.

Tom and I started to race across the playground towards the Big Toy. It was a tangle of wood and metal that had ruled our world as children. There had been rules about which grades could use it on which days because everyone wanted to play on it. I climbed to the top and looked out across the playground and the grass field. I saw the map of the U.S., the hopscotch grids, and the picnic tables where we had eaten lunch. I jumped down with a thump and walked over to the rings. I remembered Tom and the other boys used to yell at me because I took so long. That really seemed like a long time ago now. Now I could stand on the ground and reach the rings. I must be growing up, I thought.

I picked up some grayish-brown wood chips and threw them at Tom. One hit him on the back. That started a war. We dodged around the Big Toy, throwing wood chips at each other. One hit Tom on the forehead, so we decided to quit.

I looked over at the tether ball poles, which stood like guards near the multipurpose room. Tom and I ran at them fast and swung around them. I had been good at tether ball. I remember the sound of the ball hitting my hand. Amanda was the champion of the tether ball courts. Everyone wanted to beat her. I smiled at the memory of the day I did. If only the rest of life were a tether ball game.

Tom and I walked around the back of the beige multipurpose building, turned left, and raced for the kindergarten building, which was back towards the front of the school. We opened the gate and walked over to the big, floor-to-ceiling windows in the building. I shielded my eyes and looked in. I could see the brick-colored cardboard blocks and the trucks. The same brown rug was on the floor. I looked to my right and saw a smaller version of the Big Toy. I wandered over. I could easily hoist myself from the ground onto the highest platform. I laid there thinking about growing up, about how things were getting easier to do.

"Hey, Larry, let's go," called Tom.

"O.K.," I said.

Tom and I walked along quietly. I felt good about going back to my old school. Now I know for sure that I am growing up.

FIGURE 11.3. A 6 Paper: Swamp Thing

We had planned a nice day at Foothill Lake, to just sit back and relax our work-fried brains. The day was perfect. The sky was blue and clear. A light breeze blew, cooling us from the shining sun. The long-forgotten smell of seawater brought back memories of the beaches in my old hometown. It was everything I could have ever wished for. Little did I know that an event would happen that day that would forever change my life.

After eating a wonderful picnic lunch at the Oak Grove, we set off with our equipment to go to the lake. It was incredible. God's glory and creativeness in nature was all around us. We were surrounded by nothing but beauty. The sun shone on the surface of the lake in a way that made it look like liquid gold. The wind made it ripple ever so slightly, creating a glittering light show, like none created by man. The mallards swam about, going about their business, and the fish darted around, trying to avoid them. Across the lake, I could see a small island, lined with the greenest of trees, all just out of reach of the land and accessible only by boat.

We took out an inflatable boat, and my Dad brought out the foot pump. My sister and I each took turns delighting in the simple joy of stomping furiously on the pump until the boat was inflated. We put it on the water beside the dock, and my Mom and my sister took the first turn on it. After constant begging, my cousin and I got the boat. We paddled across the lake with only one thing on our mind: the island. The boat churned the water and created two long ripples behind us that trailed on for more than ten yards until dissolving back into the calm waters.

When we arrived at the island, we tied the boat and jumped onto the island. A thin dirt path snaked through the entire island. We walked slowly through it, admiring all its wonders. Small birds hopped around, collecting materials for their nests. We even saw a couple young squirrels chasing each other here and there. The one being chased would stop now and then to allow the other to catch up. It then darted back and forth, just out of range of the other, to tease him. Then the chasee took off again in a blur, leaving a swirling cloud of dirt. They continued this over and over again until one caught the other in a friendly tackle, and they rolled out of sight. We smiled to see how human-like they acted. But how did they get onto this isolated island? Squirrels don't swim, do they? Just then, the rest of my family appeared around the corner.

"Hey, old salts!" my mother chuckled.

"Hey! How'd you get here?" my cousin and I asked in unison.

"While you were off sailing the seven seas, WE took the path," my sassy sister smugly said. (I'd like to see *her* say that five times frast . . . fust . . . fivst . . . f . . . f . . . FAST! Humph.)

"Path?" I asked in disbelief.

"It was behind the island." My sister deliberately smiled. Then she put on her "I'm so cute and smart and you're not" face. I could smack her.

We spent a while on the island and then decided to return to the dock to look at the fishes. They took the path, but my cousin and I were made to paddle the boat all the way back to the dock, a journey that seemed much longer than the one coming to the island.

Back at the dock, we sat down on the edge of the dock and dipped our feet into the chilling water. Looking into the lake, we saw mostly seaweed and it took us a few minutes to catch sight of the little fish darting in and out of the swaying green masses. We suddenly felt the need to catch one, but we had no fishing pole. So, I set out to find a solution.

I always like to make things. I wandered around looking for parts to make a fishing pole to catch some fish. I found a stick for the rod and a weed stem for the line. I took a paper cup from lunch and poked holes in the bottom to form a net. I tied the weed stem to it and then to the stick and I was ready.

I looked into the water to find a good spot to fish. I saw a school of fish and ran to get my makeshift fishing apparatus. I hurried back, but I tripped and did a cartwheel into the water. It was my very first successful cartwheel, but too bad it had to be into water. I remember it as clear as day. From the moment my foot hit the rock edge, I knew I was bound for doom. As I slowly tipped over, all I could do was yell, "Whaaa-owww!" and let my arms flail helplessly through the air. I saw the water rushing up to my face and suddenly time seemed to slow down, as if to taunt me and to show me more clearly what I was in store for. Then time let go, dropping me into the freezing waters with a loud SPLASH! Water flew in practically all directions.

My mom, who had already returned from the island, came hurrying to help me. I crawled out, covered with seaweed. I thought I lost my glasses, but they were in my hand.

My dad humorously yelled, "Look! It's the Swamp Thing!"

CASE 12

Adventures in the Narrative Evaluation Jungle or, How Many Hours of Sleep Can *You* Get While Assessing?

Gwen Toevs

Is this long enough?
Was that encouraging enough?
Was that too honest?
Will I alienate the student?

These and many other questions plagued my weary brain as I plodded on through 31 narrative evaluations. It was 2:00 in the morning. I'd spent hours on evaluations during winter break, hours the previous week, and I was up against my "they can't possibly be turned out any later than Friday" deadline. I wanted my life back and I simply had to get them done. This meant typing away under that classroom fluorescence until 1:00 and 2:00 in the morning every night that week.

Time. They take so much time. I am in my fourth year of teaching multi-grade classrooms. Previously a teacher in private schools, I had done narrative evaluations before and they took forever. Of course, then I only had to do 10 and I was given paid time off to accomplish them. This time I had 31 to do and had no guidelines or stated expectations from the school. With my mentor teacher I had brainstormed ways of being efficient. At first I thought I should touch on everything each student had done. Instead, she suggested I briefly mention their strengths, challenges, and the goals I had for the next quarter. We practiced on one student and it took about three minutes. However, here I was at 2:00 A.M. and each evaluation was taking at least an hour.

I looked through their working portfolios, re-reading their work, my comments, and their self-evaluations. I looked for strengths, challenges, and goals. While trying to be brief and efficient on this journey, I felt weighed down with insecurity.

The semester had not been completely successful. I spent it scrambling for some kind of system that would work in my unique environment. I teach at a small charter middle school that serves children with special needs, those who have fallen through the cracks of regular public school, and those who simply want a smaller school environment. Of the school's 31 students, half are special education students (special day class and Resource Specialist Program [RSP]); one-third are on medication for attention deficit disorder (ADD), attention deficit hyperactivity disorder (ADHD), and manic depression/obsessive compulsion disorder; one-sixth are very gifted; and many are a few years behind on their social skills.

The school has two full-time teachers. In the morning I teach language arts to 15 students for 45 minutes, then I get the other 16 students for 45 minutes, while my co-teacher teaches math. After our break we both teach a writer's workshop, followed by physical education and lunch. In the afternoon I teach art while he teaches science and history. In a logical world I might have had the more skilled and gifted students in one language arts class, and the less skilled students in the other.

However, we did not want to segregate students whose self-esteem and social standing had already been harmed by tracking. Thus I had a mix of skills in each class that ranged from a second-grade to a tenth-grade level.

I began the year with the overly ambitious goal of doing literature circles, spelling, and centers every day of the week. I had two parent volunteers each day, and I did three lesson plans and curricular development for each level. The students were not successfully doing their homework, I did not have adequate time to train the parents or fully explain the lessons they were leading, and I was burning out from 60- and 70-hour work weeks. I tried numerous other endeavors such as reciprocal reading, spelling programs, and whole group instruction.

At the end of the semester, any kind of standardized assessment seemed impossible. The students had all done different work. Although I had graded the big projects, I had no day-to-day assessment system built in so that parents leading other groups could document accomplishments and failures. *Would the parents think I had accomplished enough with their children based on what was in their portfolio?* I was striving in these narratives to document each and every thing they had accomplished, mentioning strengths and challenges and the student's specific interest for each project.

I agonized over how to word each evaluation. I wanted to accurately assess my special education students while at the same time do some serious cheerleading. These students have had their egos crushed from almost every direction. Where before they had been assessed by teachers who compared them to regular students with grade-level skills, I wanted them to know that I saw who they were; I saw their unique skills, creativity, effort, and improvement.

While some projects sparked the interest of my gifted students, many had been doing very average work far below their capability. I wanted to thoroughly acknowledge their strengths, while at the same time diplomatically stating that they could be putting in much more effort. Ann, for example, always chose the easiest option when I gave the students choices on projects. While she turned her work in, it was simplistic and ob-

viously took her very little effort. I wanted to inspire Ann, rather than alienate her, when I wrote that as a highly gifted student in a mixed ability classroom she had the added responsibility of challenging herself. I proposed that if she could show me some serious effort and self-motivation, I would give her more rein in creating her assignments and deadlines.

My ADD/ADHD students have a much more difficult time completing assignments, staying on task, and organizing themselves. Yet I most definitely found strengths I could expound upon. "What an actor this student is! Such strong verbal skills! Incredible (non-stop) abilities in improvisation!" At the same time, I needed to acknowledge that their portfolios were practically empty. I was compelled to admonish these students to respect their classmates' right to learn in a classroom that was quiet and free of constant distraction. "Ha-ha, good luck," I chuckled to myself. These students have had behavioral problems for years. They are on medications and have been in numerous behavior modification programs at different schools. It was unrealistic to hope for change in the students merely by mentioning the need for change in their evaluation.

One student, although highly capable, had turned in nothing all semester. I focused on her marvelous compassion and social skills. She has a warm and loving way of making all students feel included. At the top of her evaluation, however, I wrote *unsatisfactory*.

When I actually succeeded at writing a brief evaluation, I scrutinized myself harder. *This is a girl's evaluation. If you don't write more about her you're discriminating against girls . . . This is a special education student's evaluation. You're discriminating against students with lower skills. Write more.*

My insecurities kept nagging at me. I felt that the students, along with their parents, were going to judge me. A student-directed, self-motivated school environment is a major goal of our charter, one I have always held dear. I believe it is most educational and empowering for the students to assess themselves, yet my attempts at including them in this process had not been very successful. I had asked them to write about three pieces in their working portfolio, explaining how this work showed effort and growth and why the student was proud of them. The students picked some of the projects I wanted to write about, but many had picked some obscure worksheet that involved little investment. While wanting to respect their choices, I was hardly going to waste a sentence on a spelling worksheet that took a student about 10 minutes. She had written 100% on the top of it, to accompany my comments (as if I wouldn't know my own handwriting!). The evidence of growth gleaned from this worksheet, the student wrote, is that she had received a 100%. I resolved that it was my job to assess the students, and it was unrealistic in a real-world setting that they would always assess themselves. Others constantly assess us for social skills and accomplishments. *Keep writing. Don't get blocked*, I told myself.

I finally finished at 3:00 in the morning on Friday. Printing out the last paper (see Figure 12.1 for two sample evaluations), I gave a deep sigh and anticipated the next day of school—just five hours away. The week had been horrible. Student behavior was shockingly bad. I was exhausted, not thoroughly prepared, and the students sensed my weakness and tried to have their way, as middle schoolers do so well. I had mentioned that I was doing their evaluations and I couldn't believe that they were behaving so poorly. When my teachers were writing evaluations and giving out grades it was a time to impress them with volunteered favors, punctuality, and completed homework. My students responded that since these evaluations were on their previous semester, their present behavior should have no influence. Furthermore, I was told, I should be objectively reporting their grades. *Isn't all assessment subjective?* From the way we grade a paper, project, or test, to the way we fudge a student's final grade with a plus or a minus? This conversation inspired me to go back and get a little more direct with my criticism on a number of students' evaluations. I think assessment is extremely subjective unless one is giving fill-in-the-bubble tests, which measure a student's ability to take that type of test as much as they measure content knowledge. Again I ask, is it *possible* to be objective when using authentic assessment?

It was time to see how the students would react to their evaluations. I wrote four prompts on the board: "I agree with . . . I disagree with . . . I think that . . ." and "I am going to try to . . ." While some students agreed with almost everything I said—their goals for the next semester being the same goals I had for them—other students disagreed with almost everything I said (except for their strengths, of course). One goal I gave Bill was to take more time to do a final proofread of his work so it was slick and legible. He responded to most of his evaluation defensively, stating in nearly undecipherable handwriting, "I have no problem getting my work in and my handwriting is just fine." Ann, one of my gifted students, responded, "It is the teacher's job to challenge me, certainly not mine. Besides, how am I supposed to get motivated when you guys are always telling me what to write? I never get to do what I want." A surprising sentence, considering that we follow Nancy Atwell's style of writer's workshop, spending considerable time helping the students brainstorm what they want to write about (Atwell, 1987).

Given the tremendous amount of painstaking work I had done, one can imagine the standing ovation, gold medals, and kudos I thought should be coming my way. A few parents thanked me for the encouragement and the way I "pegged" their child. One parent of a student who had been in special day class for years was very appreciative of all of the positive feedback I gave her son. Typically he had received Cs and Ds for his best work—and this kid works! He puts a tremendous amount of thought and effort into each assignment. So while documenting his challenges, I also praised him effusively. But aside from these few bits of positive feedback, I did not hear from most parents.

The most shocking response came from the school council a board made up of parents and staff that acts as the administration of the school. I asked for a day or two off in compensation for the 30-plus overtime hours I had worked. Eight to 16 hours off seemed like modest recompense to me. I left the council meeting so people could talk freely about my request. Reading the meeting minutes later felt like far more than a slap in the face. I felt like I had been run over by a Mack truck. "New teachers will find more efficient methods of assessment." "Time off will put a burden on the other teachers." What about the burden I had just endured? I was not given a choice about which assessment system I could use. I was simply told that we do narrative evaluations.

The adolescent in me figured out my new assessment system on the spot. *Student made good progress, or student made poor progress* would replace all of my carefully crafted evaluations. The council had decided to give us half a day off to do our final evaluations. I figured my new system would take no more than an hour and I could recoup a couple of those hours off. Yes, new teachers will indeed develop more efficient assessment systems.

The professional inside me soon returned and I began creating a standardized assessment system to accompany our new revised language arts program. I was only doing literature circles. There is so much I feel I should be teaching, but we need to focus on one thing and succeed at it before I add more. My mentor teacher brought me a stack of rubrics for different projects and it was not difficult for me to get the general sense of a rubric and brainstorm a range of skills that I wanted my students to aim for. My aide, my parent volunteers, and I keep a log for each group, checking in assignments done punctually, the quality of discussion, and the quality of written response (see Figure 12.1 for sample student evaluations). Half of my new evaluation sheet is a self-evaluation completed by the students (see Figure 12.2a and b). They read the rubrics and put a check next to anything that applies to them, then they summarize their performance with a 1, 2, 3, or 4. They write down their strengths and their goals. I complete the same information, with the addition of a section called "Ways parents/grandparents can help their students succeed" (see Figure 12.3). Over spring break I used this new system for midterms and it only took about 10 hours of my time plus one session of class time to complete.

I did, in fact, feel that this process was a fairly objective assessment involving useful student self-reflection. I simply report the work turned in and work still missing, and summarize the daily parent volunteer assessment of their group's literature discussion. My expectations are so clear to the students and myself that I feel very objective as I look over their written assignments. Individual goals come straight from the rubric. The students had no surprises when they received their new evaluation; typically their self-assessment and goals are the same if not close to my assessment of them. I do not describe their work in nearly as much detail as I did before, however.

I have always supported narrative evaluations. Grades tell very little about a student except that they can work the system, which is perhaps all that future employers will want to know. I feel that assessment should be personal and encouraging, yet realistic. Students should be evaluated on their effort, improvement, and risk-taking in comparison with their previous work. I am having serious questions, however, about the capacity of this method to motivate students to do consistently good work. Ideally, students should feel a "natural curiosity" that leads them toward new skills and information. My experience with middle school students is strikingly different. While some students would explore some subjects, most would be satisfied to socialize and play computer games.

In a regular public school, students are given one grade for a class. If they have done stellar work, it is averaged in with all the missing assignments and not so stellar work. Unless work is consistently stellar, these outstanding pieces fade into the all-encompassing averaged grade. Narrative evaluations, on the other hand, detail the stellar work and the missing work. In this way they are both more and less forgiving. My own college career was assessed with such evaluations. While my teachers documented that I had missed some assignments and had been late almost every day, they also described the outstanding work I did. If I had been given grades I might have received a B- or C once all points were taken away for tardiness and the zeros averaged in. Would I have been more accountable with a letter grade system? Would my students?

My travels through the assessment jungle have left me with many questions. Do students want their strengths and weaknesses detailed, or would they prefer the anonymity of grades? Do students and parents appreciate the tremendous amount

FIGURE 12.1. Sample Student Evaluations

Sample 1: Language Arts

Strengths: Ann is very good at expressing her opinions and using sound reasoning and evidence from the text to support them. This is evident in literature circle discussions and especially in her written test on Tom's Midnight Garden.

Ann did a thorough job researching information for her alphabet bug book. It was creative and neatly presented.

Ann is also a great helper —a much appreciated social skill at Sojourn. When other students need help she is very compassionate and patient in supporting their learning.

Weaknesses: Sometimes attitude and socializing get in the way of academics for Ann. However, when talked to Ann has been responsible and able to monitor her own behavior.

Because Ann is a highly skilled student in a mixed ability classroom, she has the added responsibility of challenging herself. Sometimes Ann does this, and sometimes I feel she is doing good work when she is capable of doing excellent work. If Ann set some goals for herself and demonstrated that she was self-motivated and good at independent work, I would give her more leeway in helping design her assignments.

Goals: In addition to the above goal, I would like to see Ann further her skills in the study of literature. As a helper and a natural leader, Ann can help herself and her group to understand the text, make connections between the text and life experience, and understand the test within its historical context. Ann can model expressing one's opinion and supporting it with evidence from the text.

Sample 2: Language Arts

Strengths: AJ's main strength is that he is a fantastic actor. His oral performances have all been excellent. His last performance—an improvised personification of a TV arguing with a remote control—was hysterical. AJ is very quick and clever. Another strength is AJ's love of poetry. As well as being a great author of poetry, he also enjoys reading and performing it. AJ has great reading skills and is capable of producing excellent work.

Weaknesses: AJ is very easily distracted. When he is upset about issues at home or school he is nearly impossible to keep on task. AJ's behavior can be very disruptive for the rest of the class.

Goals: I would like to see AJ have more respect for his and his classmates' right to learn. I would like him to make a strong effort to be respectful and focused in class. During preparation time for literature circles, I have a parent volunteer working one on one with him. I would like AJ to honor the volunteer's time by staying focused on his work. I would like AJ to practice group learning skills such as active listening, not interrupting, agreeing/disagreeing with a classmate and explaining his reasoning. I would like AJ to use his strong oral skills to help other s in his literature circle to understand the text. I know AJ will succeed if he tries hard.

FIGURE 12.2A. Written Response Rubric

#1 Each assignment is an example of my best work.

___I put a lot of thought into my work.
___I follow the guidelines of each assignment and I answer every part of the question.
___My answers include a lot of details from my life experience and from the book.
___I frequently use evidence from the book—such as quotes—to support my opinions.
___I ask questions that make people share their opinions instead of asking memory questions.
___I write my response in neat handwriting. I go back and proofread my work for punctuation and
    spelling errors.
___I ask for help when I need it.

#2 Most assignments I do are example of good work.

___I usually answer all parts of the questions, but sometimes I leave something out.
___Sometimes my answers are detailed and I use examples from my life experience and the book.
___Sometimes I use evidence from the book to support my opinions.
___I try my best to ask thinking questions, but sometimes I ask simple memory questions.
___Usually I try to write neatly, but sometimes I'm a little sloppy.
___You might find some spelling and punctuation errors in my work.
___Sometimes I ask for help when I need it.

#3 I do my work as fast as I can so I have something to turn in.

___I frequently do not answer all parts of the question.
___I write down the easiest thing I can just to get it done.
___Sometimes I include details from the book or from my life, but usually I don't.
___I ask simple memory questions and I might not be sure what a thinking question is.
___Sometimes my handwriting is neat but sometimes it is sloppy.
___Someone else would probably find spelling and punctuation errors in my work.
___I don't ask for help very much.

#4 This is definitely not my best work—I can do much better!

___I do not give complete answers to the assignment questions.
___I just write down a couple of sentences and that's enough for me.
___I usually do not have my work done on time.
___I show very little evidence from the book to support my opinions.
___I answer with almost no detail.
___If someone was reading my work, they would probably think I did not read the book.
___If you can't read my writing or pick through my spelling mistakes, tough luck!
___I don't care if I need help—just tell me when break is!

FIGURE 12.2B. Literature Circle Discussion Rubric

#1 I try really hard to help people in my group understand the book better, and to learn from their ideas.

___I share my opinions.
___I listen to others and when it is my turn I respond to what they said.
___I frequently support my opinions with examples from the book.
___I ask people for clarification when I don't understand what they said.
___When we talk about the personal experiences the book reminds us of, I help my group stay focused on the book instead of getting off task.
___I wait for my turn to talk—I am careful not to interrupt others.

#2 I participate in literature circle discussion.

___Sometimes I share my opinions.
___Sometimes I listen to others and occasionally I respond to what they said.
___Sometimes I support my opinions with information from the book.
___I might ask people to explain themselves if I do not understand what they said, but sometimes I just ignore it.
___I like to talk about personal experiences the book reminds me of, and sometimes we get off task.
___Usually I am a good listener, but sometimes I interrupt people.

#3 Sometimes I add to my group discussion, but I don't try hard.

___I usually do not like to share my work.
___I frequently ignore what others are saying and I don't try to respond.
___I say what I think but I can't tell people why I think it.
___If I don't understand what people said I rarely ask them to explain themselves.
___I definitely get off task when my group is discussing the book.
___I frequently interrupt other people because I want to say something and I don't really want to listen to them.

#4 I do not add to my literature circle discussion.

___I usually refuse to participate or answer "I don't know."
___I don't listen to what other people are saying.
___I distract other people in my group by talking about something else or I just space out and don't participate.
___I interrupt people a lot and I almost never wait for my turn.
___If someone saw me they would think I had not read the book.
___If someone saw me they would think I did not care if I and the other people in my group understood the book.

FIGURE 12.3. Sample Literature Circle Evaluation

Student Self-Evaluation:

1. I have turned in   all   most   some   (little)   (none)   (circle one) of my work **on time**.

2. Using the assessment guide Gwen gave me, the quality of my **written work** is best described by
   1   (2)   (3)   (4) (circle one).

3. Using the assessment Gwen gave me, the quality of my literature **discussion** is best described by
   (1)   2   (3)   (4) (circle one).

4. I think my work is good because _____ *I tink about how I could make it bettee* _____

   _____

5. My goals that I will focus on to improve the quality of my work are:

   1. *I will actually turn my work in finished*

   2. *I will finsh my work at home instead of school*

   3. *I will do my work befor the last minute so it is better guality*

Teacher Evaluation:

   Student turned in _7_ out of _12_ assignments on time. *2 absences*
   Student is missing _5_ assignments. *Danny has done some fabulous illustrations*
   Quality of response _2-3_. (see rubric)
   Quality of discussion _1-2_. (see rubric) *Thoughtful discussion, lots of interruptions*

   Student uses assignment book   consistently   frequently   (infrequently)   never.

   Goals for student:

   1) Write down assignments in assignment book so you do not get mixed up.

   2) Do for homework whatever you don't get done in class.

   3) Read over your work—make sure it is _readable_ *and complete.*

   Ways Parents/Grandparents can help their student succeed:

   1) Ask to see Danny's assignment book + homework _daily_

   2) Read over his work with him to be sure it is readable and complete

   3) Help Danny pace himself so he can do a little at a time instead of having to do it all at once.

Parent Signature   _____

Teacher Signature   _____

Student Signature   _____

of work that goes into crafting an evaluation? How do narrative evaluations, as opposed to letter grades, affect student output? How do our assessments make students feel about themselves? Would letter grades motivate my students when they haven't necessarily done so in regular education classrooms? Finally, are schools ready to adequately support teachers in the enormous amount of time and effort that go into narrative evaluations, or will it always be one more job teachers get to do in the wee hours of the night?

REFERENCE

Atwell, N. (1987). *In the middle: Writing, reading, and learning with adolescents.* Portsmouth, NH: Heinemann.

CHAPTER 5

Using Assessments to Guide Support for Beginning Teachers

Ellen Moir

In 1982, while working as a Supervisor of Teacher Education at the University of California, Santa Cruz, I was struck by a disturbing pattern—each year dozens of our recent graduates would call me in November, desperate for help and threatening to resign from the teaching jobs they had so recently been delighted to accept. They were clearly shocked by the discrepancy between their ideals and the reality of classroom teaching. Since I had worked closely with these new teachers over their two years of pre-service preparation, I knew they were intelligent and talented. These heart-wrenching phone calls propelled me to look for solutions that went beyond providing short-term help.

After conversations with new teachers and my university colleagues, and a review of the scant research available on the first years of teaching and mentoring support, I realized that the critical initial stage in a teacher's development had been neglected by the profession. If educators in Santa Cruz County wanted to help novice teachers overcome the challenges that were threatening to derail their careers, we would have to develop an ambitious model of support for beginning teachers. I brought together district administrators, principals, union representatives, experienced teachers, new teachers, and UC Santa Cruz Education Department faculty to design a comprehensive support program. The result was the initiation in 1988 of the Santa Cruz New Teacher Project (SCNTP), which has now supported more than 3,000 beginning teachers, and is becoming a state and national model for induction. The SCNTP's success led to the eventual creation of the New Teacher Center at the University of California, Santa Cruz, which opened in 1998.

At the heart of the Santa Cruz New Teacher Project is the conviction that experienced and talented colleagues are the most important resource for our novice teachers. Each year our participating districts release veteran teachers to work as mentors for up to 15 new teachers. Mentors are selected for their outstanding classroom practice, professional development expertise, and strong communication skills. Intensive professional development prepares mentors both to support and assess new teachers, focusing on their strengths as well as their challenges. Because advising is a full-time job for our mentors, they work with novices when they are most in need of advising, in their classrooms during the school day. Mentors respond to novice teachers' needs in all areas of practice: curriculum development, instruction, classroom management, and communication with parents and administrators. They provide the expertise and encouragement that help new teachers maintain a positive outlook and develop confidence in their capabilities despite unexpected challenges and problems. This collaborative work focuses on student learning, with particular attention being paid to building a classroom program that promotes equitable learning and the educational success of every child.

We have come to learn that this role of mentor involves learning new skills and new ways of thinking and talking about practice. As a result, one of the key features of our program is weekly professional development sessions for mentors. At these gatherings we use cases to explore the most effective strategies for helping novice teachers improve their practice. Analysis of these practical examples of mentor/novice teacher interaction has underscored that what works for new teachers in their classrooms also works for mentors. Our mentors teach novices to gather and evaluate student assessment data to continuously improve instruction. The same process works for mentors themselves, who also teach a "class of beginning teachers" whom they must systematically assess to determine the best "next steps." Mentors must be attuned to subtleties, including the teacher's background, classroom context, developmental level, and capacity to absorb feedback, as well as school/district cultures. Like classroom teachers, they have to take into account the readiness of their advisees to hear and implement their suggestions.

The following three cases, written by SCNTP mentors, tell such stories. They illustrate the range of issues that arise when mentors take their teacher role into the world of advising adults. As mentors deepen their teaching relationships with each novice and collect additional assessment data, they begin to figure out how and when to intervene. They find themselves reflecting on how practices they used as classroom teachers may or may not be appropriate to the advisor role. How are agreements made about next steps for beginning teacher learning? When does a situation call for explicit explanation, and when is a question that promotes thoughtfulness more effective?

These new teacher mentors model a variety of approaches that are used in the mentoring relationship. We see examples of reflective conversations that involve open-ended questioning. We hear about the explicit modeling of lessons. We see how mentors guide a teacher to gather data through observation of students in class, and to analyze student work. The mentors constantly question the teaching decisions they make with new teachers—what effect did the coaching strategies have on the beginning teacher's practice? Just as effective classroom teachers frequently assess what students are learning and adjust instruction to meet their evolving needs, effective mentors base their next steps on careful assessment of novices' evolving practice.

These cases are, in fact, an instructional tool for all teachers because they bring up themes that address our current professional dilemmas. The challenge is great for teachers to implement content area standards, evaluate student work, and differentiate instruction appropriately. For a beginning teacher who is also learning to set up and manage a classroom environment for the first time and develop his or her own repertoire of teaching plans, the challenge can be overwhelming. These cases show how mentoring is an effective tool to address this problem. For the profession as a whole, the future of teaching and learning rests on our ability to assess what happens daily in our classrooms, and to communicate what we know about effective teaching to a wider audience of educators, parents, and policymakers. Cases such as these can be a compelling vehicle for transmitting best practices within and beyond the teaching profession.

CASE 13

Is Authentic Assessment Really Ideal for Grading and Reporting?

Leslie Smith

It seems on the surface that many of the problems teachers face have to do with either a scarcity of time and money, or an overabundance of bureaucracy. The idealist in me wonders what the perfect assessment program could accomplish without any of these constraints. What would we have to include in its design? The pragmatist in me asks, "Are there any pitfalls inherent in authentic assessment? Are there pedagogical tensions that inevitably would arise?"

This past year, I've had the opportunity to examine these questions from a new vantage point. I have been released from teaching sixth graders to work as a Beginning Teacher Support and Assessment (BTSA) support provider, serving a total of 15 new teachers at seven elementary and middle school sites. I meet weekly with each of my first- and second-year teachers to problem-solve, focus on increasing student achievement, and document their progress.

In our work with new teachers, we use the California Standards for the Teaching Profession (CSTP) to provide feedback and track teachers' progress. When it comes to Standard #6, Assessing Student Learning, Gwen was my star. She began her second year of public school teaching at a practically brand-new charter middle school with a total student population that hovered around 30. Her students' families had chosen a small charter school in hopes of finding a program tailored to supporting students' social and academic needs. When Gwen arrived, there weren't any guidelines, expectations, or policies to inform her decisions about assessment. She was basically at liberty to create a program. Fortunately, as a result of her teacher credential program and her prior teaching experience, Gwen already had a solid understanding of authentic assessment. From observing her at the beginning of the year, I was confident that Gwen would flourish as she developed systems to capture student growth, inform her instruction, and inspire ongoing improvement. I looked forward to working with her.

In the fall, Gwen implemented several assessments: writing rubrics, a system to monitor student performance in literature studies, student self-assessment and goal-setting, and frequent parent conferences. Occasionally we brainstormed ways for her to refine her use of these tools. What really impressed me about Gwen was that she used her assessments to make sound decisions about instruction and materials. She selected literature studies choices that reflected her students' reading levels and interests. An instructional aide used guided reading with emerging readers. Vocabulary and word study were targeted at each student's developmental level. Gwen's mini-lessons in writer's workshops pinpointed skills that her students were on the verge of using correctly. During revision conferencing, Gwen used rubric categories such as "organization," "voice," and "mechanics" to focus her instruction.

The one element descriptor from the CSTP that we hadn't addressed directly was "Communicating with students, families and other audiences about student progress." So, before Gwen's first round of report cards, I wasn't surprised when this issue emerged. "Leslie," she queried, "I don't know how I am going to get these report cards done. It's a ton of work. We have decided to write narrative evaluations for each student, rather than assign letter grades. I don't know how I'll be able to teach during the day and meet this deadline."

I responded, "You know your students really well. I bet that you could tell me, without even looking at your gradebook, the specific achievements, challenges and needs you have observed among each of your students." Gwen proceeded to do just that, recounting her keen observations of one student's work during the first semester. We talked a bit more about how some parents might interpret the subtle difference between words such as "outstanding" and "excellent." Given that most students in her school had received letter grades in the past, we both imagined that parents might translate "outstanding" as an "A-plus" and "excellent" as an "A."

I left our meeting feeling confident that Gwen would be able to finish the other 29 evaluations in not more than three hours. I also reflected briefly about my own teaching background. In 15 years of evaluating student work, I had always taught in schools that relied on letter grades to report student progress. While our report cards had a small space for narrative comments, I actually hadn't ever needed to follow the advice that I had shared with Gwen. In conjunction with all the formative assessments I used in my classroom, I had always figured that letter grades and my brief remarks were sufficient.

When I met with Gwen the following week, she looked surprisingly run down. I quickly found out the source of her disillusionment. "The narratives took you 30 hours to complete? I am so sorry! The students weren't appreciative? What happened?" Immediately, I felt guilty as an advisor. How could I have prepared her better for the task? What could she have done differently? This was not the ideal assessment program after all.

As our conversation continued, I read some of the narratives and began to see the painstaking nature of her efforts. For each student, Gwen had written a two-page narrative based on their work. In evaluating Lisa's work, a student who had many absences and incomplete assignments, Gwen was able to focus on positive goals, stating,

> I would like Lisa to make a strong effort to attend class consistently and punctually. I have assigned her an advanced, adult text to read in the hope that she will engage with it and do her literature journal assignments. I have also arranged a literature circle group that is all girls. Many of the issues the book raises are quite relevant to girls today. I would like Lisa to make a serious effort to be prepared and to participate in discussion. Not only will she learn, but she will also help others in her group learn by sharing her insights and life experiences.

As her advisor I responded, "This is amazing work. You are so specific and diplomatic. I can't believe you gave this much personal attention to each of your students. At the moment, I am not seeing any shortcuts or solutions. No wonder you are so tired. I am sure the students really appreciated your effort."

Gwen proceeded to tell me that many of her students were defensive about the wording of their evaluations. One student, in practically indecipherable printing, refuted the evidence found in his portfolio stating, "I disagree that I don't make my projects neat and thorough. And my handwriting is just fine. It doesn't matter there are people who can't read it. I have a perfectly fine time finishing stuff." In response to Gwen's evaluation, another student wrote, "I think that my so called 'lack of ideas' is not my fault. If I am always told what I can and cannot write about, how can I come up with my own ideas? As for whether my ideas are good or not, that is up to the individual reader." Gwen had already provided this feedback informally during the semester, yet the "official" narratives seemed to provoke their ire.

As I read Gwen's students' feedback, I began to question the rationale for all her late nights, especially when the students were not receptive. After all, there certainly are less time consuming ways to record information about student progress. As Gwen's support provider, I have seen weekly evidence that she holds her students accountable for their work, and that their progress receives ongoing attention. After all of Gwen's work, I am frustrated about this "reporting of assessment information." Maybe students would find more inspiration and be less contentious if Gwen assigned letter grades.

Trying to take charge of the time/money pressure that had emerged, Gwen asked her parent council for additional financial compensation for her work on assessment. She learned that this type of request was not part of the budget. Gwen is hoping to have minimum days in the spring during the next round of evaluations. The administrator at the school has told her to solve the problem by not working so hard. Meanwhile, we agree that she should fashion narratives that are an approximate transcription of her rubric scores and

anecdotal records, rather than compose original writing for each student.

Nevertheless, the whole experience leaves me feeling uneasy. Was she unrealistic to expect that her students would respond favorably to the feedback she crafted so carefully? Why aren't they using her feedback to improve their work? Should I have suggested shortcuts from the outset, or was it inevitable that narrative assessments require a time commitment above and beyond our teaching responsibilities? How could I have supported Gwen so that she would feel more successful?

Ironically, this sense of disequilibrium is data for me as I assess my own work as a support provider. I have realized that I, too, need to be more systematic in tracking the development and growth of my advisees. I see a pattern emerging: My questions about authentic assessment frame my teaching and coaching as I move forward. As my practice improves, I am certain that I will continue to uncover new pedagogical complexities embedded in authentic assessment.

CASE 14

Knowing What You Want Is the First Step to Getting There

Wendy Baron

Last week in our weekly new teacher-advisor meeting, Ana and I looked at the finished student projects from the Redwood Ecology Unit. We intended to assess the quality of the students' work and their understanding of the concepts taught. It was disappointing. Most of the projects reflected lots of artistic effort, and little learning about the history and ecology of the Redwood Forest.

"What did you want your students to learn through each of these Redwood Ecology inquiries?" I asked.

"I'm not sure," Ana replied. "I've never done this before." I have been an advisor with the Santa Cruz New Teacher Project for 11 years, mentoring new teachers. I meet with each new teacher in my caseload for one and a half hours per week. I also coordinate professional development activities for the beginning teachers and advisors in the project. Typically, a new teacher and I will work together over a two-year period, spending much time during the first year on classroom management, planning, and assessing student work. Ana is a first-year teacher, a University of California, Santa Cruz credential program graduate, who is teaching a fifth-grade Structured English Immersion (SEI) class. It is January, and Ana has just returned from one week of Outdoor School with her students and is regrouping after her third bout of illness this year.

After looking at the student projects, I knew we had to do some serious work around setting expectations for student learning and supporting students through scaffolding to get there. It seemed as though Ana was unsure of what to expect from students until after their work was handed in. That afternoon, we spent several hours looking at the student projects, talking about how we might raise the quality of student work with expectations stated at the outset. We also discussed the dilemma of students' varying reading and basic academic abilities. This class of 29 fifth graders, with 6 English language learners and 11 Title I and Resource students, poses great dilemmas around setting expectations and finding appropriate reading materials and resources so all can be challenged *and* successful. Being a first-year teacher, Ana has few resources and books at her fingertips to meet the varying needs of her students. I bring whatever resources I can get my hands on, and still we struggle. In addition, some typical first-year teacher management issues make it difficult to get high-quality work from the students, who are very involved in talking to one another socially during independent work time. Keeping the class on task is challenging for Ana.

As we closed our conference, I asked if we might continue to focus on expectations for student work next week. Ana, committed to improving her students' learning and her teaching, readily agreed. She asked if I could also help with the socializing students were doing during work time. "How would it be if I came in during a lesson," I suggested, "observed the students doing some independent work and then afterwards, we talked about the lesson in relation to their behavior and the work they generated?" I left knowing I would observe during social studies time next Wednesday afternoon, and I looked forward to what we would discover.

I showed up at the appropriate time during a lesson on Colonial America. Students were in small groups using Reciprocal Teaching, a comprehension strategy (see Figure 14.1), to read the text. Since we had discussed the issue of students being social during work time, I decided to capture information about their behavior using a seating chart and coding system. I wondered if I would find a relationship between their attention to the task and the quality of their work. I quickly set out to sketch a room arrangement that would allow me to code what each group was doing. I began doing 3-minute sweeps noting the group behaviors. I also made some comments about individual students when I noticed a particular behavior that might be interesting to discuss with Ana later.

I was surprised that all students were either reading silently or following along as one person read aloud. Just about everyone was on task, or so it seemed. During my third sweep, I helped a group get back on track with the Reciprocal Teaching process. About 10 minutes into the observation, it dawned on me that it was *too* quiet. I wasn't hearing the usual conversations I'd come to expect with Reciprocal Teaching. That's when I decided to stop recording student behavior and check in regarding the procedures I knew students were supposed to be following.

I sat in with a group of students I knew quite well. I intervened gently, "Excuse me, would you please tell me at what points you stop and use Reciprocal Teaching? I notice you've gone through three pages and I haven't heard any clarification of vocabulary, discussion, summarizing, or predicting. When does that happen?"

"Oh, we don't need to do that. We all get it," was the response from one of the most successful students in the class.

"How do you know?" I replied. *I* knew that Bill, in particular, must be having a great deal of difficulty with this text, and although he was plowing ahead with the reading, I suspected he had

gotten little meaning from the chapter. I stayed with this group and persisted.

"Who's the 'teacher' for this section?" I asked. After one student identified herself as the "teacher," I continued. "Okay, let's try it and see what happens. Would you please ask the group if they have any words that need clarifying?"

Pretty soon, "indentured servant," "House of Commons," and a variety of other words surfaced. We defined them, using the context and text dictionary.

"What do you do next?" I asked the student who was "teacher" for this round.

"Who's got a question?" she asked the group. She knew the process, and now was taking her role seriously. We had a very interesting conversation about indentured servants and slavery and the difference between the two. Finally, with prompting from the "teacher," one student volunteered to summarize the reading and another predicted what was going to happen next.

Before returning to the text, I sought feedback regarding the value of this process. "How has the Reciprocal Teaching process helped your understanding of this section?"

"I really didn't get what was going on before, and now I do," replied Bill. "Even though I'd rather just read, I liked doing it and learned more," replied another.

I looked up and noticed Ana watching. I included her in our conversation, and moved us toward setting an explicit expectation for the students. "Ms. K., how far should students read before stopping to use the Reciprocal Teaching process?"

"After each section," she replied. "Notice the titles in bold print. Read until the next title." The students seemed satisfied. We left them after we established who would be the "teacher" and where they were going to stop and do the next check in.

Ana and I spoke for a few moments about her expectations regarding use of the Reciprocal Teaching format. She had introduced students to the process by modeling it with the class, and this was their first independent use of it. We discussed how to intervene with groups so that everyone would use the process congruently. We agreed to put my observing aside so we could meet with

FIGURE 14.1. Reciprocal Teaching

Definition

Reciprocal teaching refers to an instructional activity that takes place in the form of a dialogue between teachers and students regarding segments of text. The dialogue is structured by the use of four strategies: predicting, clarifying, question generating, and summarizing. The teacher and students take turns assuming the role of teacher in leading this dialogue.

Purpose

The purpose of reciprocal teaching is to facilitate a group effort between teacher and students as well as among students in the task of bringing meaning to the text. Each strategy was selected for the following purpose:

Predicting

When students make predictions, they hypothesize what the author will discuss next in the text. In order to do this successfully, students must activate the relevant background knowledge that they already possess regarding the topic. The students have a purpose for reading: to confirm or disprove their hypotheses. Furthermore, the opportunity has been created for the students to link the new knowledge they will encounter in the text with the knowledge they already possess. The predicting strategy also facilitates use of text structure as students learn that headings, subheadings, and questions imbedded in the text are useful means of anticipating what might occur next.

Clarifying

Clarifying is an activity that is particularly important when working with students who have a history of comprehension difficulty. These are students who may believe that the purpose of reading is saying the words correctly; they may not be particularly uncomfortable that the words and in fact the passage are not making sense. When the students are asked to clarify, their attention is called to the fact that there may be many reasons why text is difficult to understand (e.g., new vocabulary, unclear referent words, and unfamiliar and perhaps difficult concepts). They are taught to be alert to the effects of such impediments to comprehension and to take the necessary measures to restore meaning (e.g., reread, ask for help).

Question Generating

Question generating reinforces the summarizing strategy and carries the learner one more step along in the comprehension activity. When students generate questions, they first identify the kind of information that is significant enough to provide the substance for a question. They then pose this information in a question form and self-test to ascertain that they can indeed answer their own question. Question generating is a flexible strategy to the extent that students can be taught and encouraged to generate questions at many levels. For example, some school situations require that students master supporting detail information; others require that the students be able to infer or apply new information from text.

Summarizing

Summarizing provides the opportunity to identify and integrate the most important information in the text. Text can be summarized across sentences, across paragraphs, and across the passage as a whole. When the students first begin the reciprocal teaching procedure, their efforts are generally focused at the sentence and paragraph levels. As they become more proficient, they are able to integrate at the paragraph and passage levels.

---

groups and reinforce the Reciprocal Teaching process. I sat in next with a group of Spanish readers who were still making their way through the text. I waited patiently while each student took his or her turn reading a paragraph. They knew to stop at the end of the section, and the "teacher" asked if anyone had words to clarify. No one did. He next asked for questions. There was a long pause of silence. No one ventured a question. I finally asked, "What is life like in Virginia for the colonists?" No one responded. I drew their attention back to a specific paragraph, written by a famous novelist, and asked someone to read it aloud. When she was finished, I rephrased the question, "What is this paragraph saying about people's health?" A student replied, "They are sick." I continued, "What was making them sick?" "Mosquitoes," came the answer. The "teacher" moved us along, asking if someone would summarize. The student volunteer recounted our brief discussion about mosquitoes causing sickness in Virginia. No one had a prediction for the next section until I suggested we look at the title and pictures in the next section for ideas. I knew Ana and I would have a rich discussion later on Reciprocal Teaching and other specific strategies that would support students in comprehending the text.

After reading the chapter, students were asked to write about what they had learned. While students were writing, I began thinking about the various things I had observed, and what questions and suggestions I might make. The recurring challenge for Ana seemed to be around setting clear expectations for student behavior, learning, and work products and then systematically supporting students to achieve the intended outcomes. I knew it would be important for Ana to reteach the Reciprocal Teaching process by modeling and practicing each discreet skill and role. I realized that some students needed more scaffolding in order to be successful and that a process to ensure equity of participation was needed. Finally, I understood the importance of matching the assessment tool with what Ana wanted the students to know and be able to do. In this case, it was clarifying vocabulary, generating and discussing questions, summarizing sections, and predicting what would happen next.

We began our reflecting conference by talking about the lesson in general. Ana was very pleased with her students' behavior, so we looked at the observation data for evidence of success first. It seemed that most groups were on task during the observation period, and socializing was at a minimum within each group. I used the data to lead us into a discussion about the Reciprocal Teaching process itself as well as the group using the Spanish text.

"Would you tell me a little more about your decision for using Reciprocal Teaching today?" Ana knew Reciprocal Teaching to be a comprehension strategy for use with nonfiction text. Her district had sent her to a Reciprocal Teaching workshop, where she observed modeling of the process and felt confident it would support her own students in understanding the social studies text, which was difficult reading for many. I continued, "What did you want to see students doing during the small group work?" Ana clarified that she expected her students to stop periodically and go through the format, with the "teacher" role rotating after each section. We used the observation data to talk about student use of the strategy. We noticed that two groups had tried using the strategy with little success. We talked about my intervention with a group during my fourth sweep. Ana said she appreciated the opportunity to observe how I worked with the group, guiding them in the use of the strategy and leaving them with an expectation for next steps. She used the same procedure as she worked with other groups, and found that students knew what to do, but hadn't been doing it. We were troubled, however, by the fact that the Spanish reading group, in which students could read the text and follow the Reciprocal Teaching format, might not have discussed, summarized, and predicted without teacher assistance. I talked about the scaffolding I had done, drawing students' attention to one paragraph to discuss, and using the section title and pictures to help them predict. From that conversation, we decided it was necessary to revisit and practice the roles as well as teach the discreet skills needed for each part of the process, i.e., selecting and defining vocabulary, developing discussion questions, summarizing, and predicting. Ana proposed teaching the scaffolding strategies I had used with the Spanish readers to the whole class during a lesson on "predicting." I suggested using a worksheet aligned with Reciprocal Teaching that doubles as an assessment tool to support students in using the process correctly and developing each of the discreet skills (see Figure 14.2).

We decided to look at the students' writing next. "You asked your students to write about what they learned. What are you expecting in these papers?" I asked.

Ana knew, in general, which students would remember details and write about them in complete sentences, and she predicted which students would have written little or nothing. She was unsure of what specifically they might have learned or what she should want them to learn. "There is so much information in the chapter. What is realistic, especially with the range of languages and abilities in my class?" Again, the issue of expectations for student work emerged.

So we began by loosely sorting the students' work into three piles—those on the far left were papers with the least amount of writing, those on the far right were the most complete and seemed to capture big ideas, and those in the middle included more facts than the papers on the left, but less than those on the right.

As we looked at them more carefully, Ana noticed that the student papers on the far right included many key concepts from the chapter, written in detail and approximate sequence in order of events. Student papers in the middle also included facts from the chapter, but Ana noticed many had added anecdotal stories about Pocahontas from the literature book she was reading to the whole class. The student papers on the left included one to three facts. Only one Spanish speaker turned in a paper, and he wrote about the famous novelist whose paragraph we discussed.

As we moved to closure in our conversation, we summarized our learnings and next steps. Ana would first plan a series of lessons to teach each of the discreet comprehension skills. Then she would reintroduce the roles by practicing with a new piece of text. I would bring the Reciprocal Teaching worksheet to use with the lessons, and reiterated how great it will be to have an assessment tool that is matched with the Reciprocal Teaching process. We agreed to look at student work again in a few weeks. Ana also thought she would go to our local educator supply store to find resources and reading materials to supplement the text.

I left that afternoon thinking about the students needing more assistance to access the grade-level material. Discussing scaffolding in greater depth would support Ana's second language learners. I am confident that teaching each skill and using the Reciprocal Teaching Outline will help students be more successful. But I'm still wondering how I might support Ana in setting realistic yet high expectations for student learning, work products, and behavior *before* going into a lesson or unit of study. Continuing to plan together and talking explicitly about learning goals and assessment will help. Looking at student work regularly will assist us in meeting the learning needs of the students. And then there's modeling. Our project offers new teachers release time to observe veteran teachers. Maybe she'd be interested in observing a fifth-year teacher we both know who is masterful at getting high-quality work from her very diverse class.

The following week, Ana is excited about the opportunity to observe in Sylvia's class. "And, can you do a lesson with my class? I'd love to see you model setting clear expectations with my students." I immediately agreed, glad for the opportunity to think through with her how I might do that. After all, a picture is worth a thousand words.

FIGURE 14.2. Reciprocal Teaching Outline

Name_____   Date_____

Complete the following steps with the pages you have been assigned.

I am reading from (title of book):_____
The pages I am reading are _____

Predict

What will the reading be about? What new information may be given? Answer in complete sentences!

_____

_____

_____

Read

Clarify

Are there words or thoughts (that you have had during the reading) that need to be clarified? Write them down and find out what they mean.

_____

_____

_____

_____

Questions

Ask two *input/fact* questions (the answer is in the book) on ideas and information in the reading. Use who, what, when, and where words to help ask the questions.

_____

_____

_____

_____

The Starting Point

Lori Helman

If a man will begin with certainties, he shall end in doubts; but if he will be content to begin with doubts, he shall end in certainties.

—Francis Bacon,
The Advancement of Learning

I read a newspaper article the other day that quoted a master pianist as saying, "I still enjoy teaching the beginner." I must feel the same way, because I have spent 16 of the last 20 years teaching young students at the beginning of their elementary school paths, and for the past three years I have been working with new teachers at the beginning of their careers. How interesting that many of the same questions and concerns about assessment and facilitating learning come up in both of these very different contexts.

Rebecca is a kindergarten teacher I work with who is in her second year of teaching. She shares a classroom with a veteran teacher of many years, also new to the school. It is a gray day in February when I walk into Rebecca's kindergarten classroom, yet I become charged with excitement. There's a lot going on here. Students are working actively at tables in small groups. There is a teacher-directed table where students are reading a simple little book and then using cards to reorganize common sentences. Another table finds students writing in their journals using their own developmental spelling. A third table is doing a thematic art project, and a fourth is making a take-home book related to the season. There is a word wall posted with words the students can now read by sight, and charts of messages that have been constructed by the group. An alphabet with associated pictures is posted prominently.

My job is to support and assess new teachers. I have met with Rebecca weekly for the past year and a half both during and after school. We have planned together, I have given her observational feedback on her teaching, and I have modeled specific lessons. She has attended workshops and seminars that I presented. Today when I meet with Rebecca after school she asks, "Will you look at the assessments I just did with my class? Taylor and Marisha still can't hear or make rhyming words. I am really concerned. How am I going to get them to the standards by June?"

Together we look at the data she has collected from the Language Arts assessment. "What do you notice about Taylor and Marisha as you do lessons in the class?" I ask.

"Taylor tends to be quiet and hangs back in the group. Marisha talks about things that don't relate to the lesson." We both ask questions and suggest possible actions over the next few minutes. How can she help them reach the standard? What lessons will support them to get there? What extra resources can be added to help them to succeed? After about 15 minutes I write down the next steps Rebecca will try before we meet again next week. She will organize groups based on literacy needs at the teacher table. During Taylor and Marisha's group, Rebecca will do rhyming and phonemic awareness games at their skill level. She will use rhyming books in shared reading lessons. Rebecca expresses relief that she has some specific ideas to try to help Taylor and Marisha. For her, assessment and standards are becoming integrated into teaching practice.

The next day I visit Jill's kindergarten classroom. I am energized to be here as well, because there is a happy buzz of activity. Jill is in her second year of teaching. She too shares her classroom with a veteran teacher of many years. One difference from Rebecca's situation is that Jill's partner has been in her kindergarten classroom for a long period of time. Jill's partner teacher has a structure that has been in place for 20 years. The perception in the partnership is that Jill will be a competent teacher when she can do it "just like the veteran." She has materials, a plan, and routines that she expects Jill to follow.

The students here are active and social. They are in the middle of a 45-minute free-choice activity time. Several students are playing with puzzles or drawing. Others are building with construction toys. When it is time for small group table jobs, students do an art project or a math manipulative station, or draw a picture and dictate a story to the teacher. As they finish, they move to another table or pick a "free choice." The room displays many art projects the students have done. In terms of literacy, there are no word walls, shared messages, or alphabets visible for student access. The students are happy with the activities, but their learning is not leading toward accomplishing goals set in the district literacy standards.

When I meet with Jill after school, she doesn't have a lot of questions.

"How are things going?" I ask.

"Fine, pretty well," she says.

Jill's veteran teacher partner has the year planned out. During our half-year of work together, Jill has expressed an interest in trying out the ideas she learned in her teacher education program or at recent inservices. "I don't know if that would be okay with my partner," she wonders. "She has strong ideas about how she wants things to be."

When Jill has tried new literacy strategies in the past, her co-teacher has said things like, "Kindergarten should be a time for learning through play," or "The students aren't ready for academics yet."

I ask Jill to get out her literacy assessment results. "Let's look at who is doing well and who your target students are." When we notice some specific students, such as Veronica, who are not progressing toward the standard, Jill expresses concern, but doesn't feel she has the power to change the way the class is organized.

My conversations with Jill become more explicit and less open-ended as I ask directive questions such as, "What can we do to support Veronica, whose literacy scores have remained flat since the last assessment period?" or "Let's think of a way to carve out a little time to work with specific students in groups designed to address the needs we saw in their assessment results." Jill seems interested. Maybe this conversation will take us to a next step. I find that Jill's teaching practice relies on "the way things have been" in that classroom. I volunteer to come in the following week and model a lesson that would support Veronica and her peers in learning some standards-based skills.

Jill and Rebecca get me thinking about my values as a teacher. I believe that a key ingredient to helping someone move forward, whether that someone is a student or a teacher, is knowing where to start. How do we meet a person at their level of understanding in order to expand on that knowledge? A first step is assessing where our "student" is. What does she know? What is she already able to do in this area?

I am in my third year as an advisor with the Santa Cruz New Teacher Project. Our project helps first- and second-year teachers with a support provider (advisor) who comes into a beginning teacher's class every week to talk, listen, observe, share, model, and help. It was strange for me to leave my own classroom to take on the role of new teacher support provider—no longer was there a group of 30 students to greet me every day and call me "teacher." No longer was my world limited to the four walls of my classroom and what magic I might be able to create there. Now my classroom includes my whole district, and my "students" are the new teachers I support.

Over the past three years, I have watched amazing things happen with the beginning teachers I have supported. After two years in the New Teacher Project, many of these beginners not only have become excellent teachers, but also have taken on leadership roles in their schools and districts. In a time of great change in terms of reading instruction, many of these new teachers have been on the forefront of implementing research-based effective literacy practices and leading grade-level literacy discussions. The collaborative structure they experienced in the project, as well as our district focus on standards, are indeed impacting many teachers' practice.

Using the results of assessment to guide instruction is something most teachers would agree to in principle. Of course we shouldn't spend 26 weeks teaching a "letter of the week" if our students already know their letters and sounds. Of course we should provide young readers with books at their instructional level once they begin sounding out simple words and learning a basic sight vocabulary. Our instruction has to connect with the level and needs of our students, right?

In reality, it is not as simple as all that. Veteran and new teachers who in principle support assessment-based instruction are often not able to make this a reality in their own classrooms. Teachers ask themselves: How do I get the time to assess formally and informally on a regular basis? What do I do with students who are above or behind the rest of the group? What about the traditional grade-level curriculum and "cute projects" that may not relate to goals and standards that the teacher next door is doing? Won't the parents in my class be upset if I don't do the traditional curriculum? Why should I make my professional life harder than it needs to be?

Individual differences between teachers also stand out. What has made it so easy for Rebecca to be open to an assessment-based instruction model? How can I support Jill's growth without invalidating her veteran teacher partner? Is personality an issue here, or power? If Rebecca and Jill were to be suddenly switched to the other's situation, would their behaviors still be the same? What is it about these two environments that encourage or stymie the change process?

Both teachers are new and in kindergarten. They both share their classrooms with veteran teachers. The language arts assessment program

and a standards-based instructional approach are new experiences for both of them. Jill and Rebecca are in the same district, so the expectations at that level are the same. They both have principals who want assessment-based instruction to occur. What is the difference, then?

Jill has less teacher training—just this year completing her coursework—so possibly that makes her less secure in her opinions. She has received new teacher support for less than a year. Would it have made a difference for her to be assisted during that crucial first year? Her veteran partner has been in the same location for a number of years and has an exploratory philosophy of teaching that is in sharp contrast to our academic, assessment-based literacy program. Perhaps Jill feels that she is just a visitor in someone else's home and must adapt her instructional strategies accordingly. What does this mean for my role as Jill's advisor? Must I take on the house guest role as well?

Mentoring new teachers into the profession is such an important task. The first couple of years of a new teacher's career can set the tone and personal expectations for the rest of her teaching life. What if the informal mentors, such as the veteran partner teachers, create by example or domination a new generation of status quo teachers? How will we accomplish goals that break the norm, such as having high expectations for all students?

All of this wondering leads me to question my own role as an advisor. Is my classroom bigger than my own set of new teachers? Might it also include their partners? If I expect my new teachers to use assessment-based instruction, how do I use it with them?

The more I think through Rebecca's and Jill's stories, the more connections I see between classroom teaching and new teacher advising. At first glance, we want adults to be at a readiness level for changing and growing in any area. Yet every person will come to the learning process at a slightly different starting point. Rebecca jumps on the horse at full speed. As she gallops along she hollers, "Is this the right direction?" Jill, on the other hand, has gotten on a tried and true mare that follows the same trail by the hour. In order to break away and gain momentum, she will need guidance and confidence. At first she will need to try out some trails that don't stray far off. As an advisor, how can I be her guide and assure her that the path is safe?

Not all of my new teachers will come to me with the same readiness. They will not all be easy to nudge along on the road to new learning. But wherever they are coming from, I want them to reach the same standards in the end. Like any good teacher, I have set goals for our work to-gether. I cannot change their context; I can only change what I give them and what happens in our time together. My goal at first was for Jill to use assessment-driven instruction. Now I wonder how assessment-driven instruction can become a goal in my own practice. It seems that the key to my work is finding the right place to start. Funny, I am feeling more and more like a classroom teacher again all the time.

CHAPTER 6

Working with Case Writers:
A Methodological Note

Judith H. Shulman

In earlier writings, I briefly examined the iterative process used in working with teachers to write cases and analyzed the impact the process had on their practice (Shulman, 1991; Shulman & Kepner, 1999). In this methodological note, I provide a more detailed description of our case development process, focusing specifically on the cases in this volume. We invite readers interested in working with practitioners to develop their own cases to use and/or to adapt any of the methods described in this chapter.

GETTING STARTED

After reviewing the case literature and finding a glaring gap on student assessment, I embarked on a journey to create a casebook to fill that gap. I was particularly interested in developing cases within classrooms that used standards-based instruction. For most teachers, employing assessments in such classrooms is relatively new, yet many school reforms require that teachers develop and use them appropriately with their students.

My first task was to select a co-editor with more expertise than I on assessment. Just as in a case discussion where we seek multiple perspectives on issues embedded in the narrative, the same is true during case development. For this volume, I served as the expert on case development and Andrea Whittaker as the expert on assessment.[1]

Our first task was to design a set of guidelines for the casebook. To help with this task, we gathered a group of educators knowledgeable about assessment and asked: "What challenges and/or

dilemmas do we want this casebook to illustrate?" Put another way: What would these narratives be "cases of"? Then we designed a set of descriptors and writing prompts for each topic, such as "Designing, using, and capturing assessments that capture student learning" and "Incorporating assessments into instruction," and incorporated these into the "Guidelines for Writing Cases" (see Appendix A).

The next task was to select a group of case writers who worked in schools implementing standards-based instruction and were interested in spending time grappling with the challenges of assessment. Since this project was initiated by a grant from the National Partnership for Excellence and Accountability in Teaching (NPEAT), we asked NPEAT partners for recommendations and were referred to two networks: 1) the Joint Venture: Silicon Valley Network, which consists of Bay Area teachers who met monthly, and 2) the New Teacher Project, located at the University of California, Santa Cruz. We piloted our methods with a small group of teachers from the former and worked with a larger group from the latter.

Drafting the Cases

Introductory seminar.[2] We begin with a two-day seminar that introduces authors to our conception of dilemma cases and gets them started on drafting their narratives. Many teachers with whom we work have not written any formal materials since they left college or university, so we take care to sequence a set of activities that introduces case writing in a safe and supportive environment.

After preliminary introductions, which set the stage for a supportive learning community, we engage the teachers in a case discussion using a narrative from a previous casebook. Our purpose here is to introduce the value of cases and case discussion as tools for professional development. During a debriefing after the discussion, we analyze both the structure and content of the case as narrative and examine the teaching note from the *Facilitator's Guide*. We want authors to get a sense of the kind of guidance potential case discussion facilitators can get from these materials.

Next, we examine the guidelines for the casebook and deliberate about what kinds of classroom episodes would illustrate the topics in the guidelines. During this discussion, case writers begin to describe what they might want to write about, and we ask, "Would this be a good case?" By that we mean, does this particular story make a theoretical claim that it is a case "of" something, or an instance of a larger class? For instance, after one teacher described a variety of problems she encountered while developing narrative evaluations for her students' report cards, I asked questions such as, "Does this story ring true?" "Will teachers identify with it?" "Are these kinds of problems typical for teachers who use narrative evaluations?" When the answer was "yes," I said that this story or "case seed" could potentially develop into a good teaching case. As noted in the Preface, "To be valuable as a case . . . the narrative should be representative of a class or type of dilemma, problem, or quandary that arises with some frequency in teaching situations."

When we feel that participants have an idea of what they want to write about, we engage them in a 10-minute free-write activity, suggesting that they write nonstop about their chosen topic without being concerned about the quality of their writing. When the time is up, we ask them to read what they've written, underline key ideas, and take three more minutes to elaborate on *one* idea. Then we divide the group into pairs, asking one person to present his or her case seed and the other person to take the role of active listener and raise questions. After both partners get a chance to discuss their respective stories, we debrief again as a group. Most people find this activity a help-

ful and safe way to start the writing process. Then we ask participants to spend the next few hours writing on their own, elaborating on their "seeds" using feedback from their partner. Some leave this first day saying, "I now know what I really want to write about," and go off to draft a story from a different classroom episode.

The following morning, they return to the group with four copies of their new drafts, and spend the morning—in groups of four—sharing their narratives with colleagues according to a list of questions intended to scaffold the conversation. Each person has approximately 30 minutes to discuss their draft. After lunch, we debrief the process, list the themes of their cases on chart paper, and discuss how they relate to one another. We also discuss how to craft their narratives into a teaching case, and often use a participant's case seeds as an example. When we adjourn, most participants have a pretty good idea of how to write their first draft. However, phone calls and/or e-mail messages often go back and forth between authors and editors in response to questions.

First drafts. When the drafts are completed, the editors meet together to discuss each one and agree on the kind of feedback we want to provide (e.g., clarifications, suggested additions, questions, and so forth). Based on this discussion, one of us prepares written comments for each case, structured by questions on a review form. The questions include:

- What was effective about the case?
- What needs clarification or elaboration?
- Do you have suggestions about the style or structure of this piece?
- Are there ways to improve the beginning or ending of the case?
- Do you think the beginning draws someone into the case quickly?
- Does the ending spark discussion naturally?
- What is this a case of?

We all gather again for a follow-up session, during which much of the time is spent working within the same small group settings used during the seminar. To prepare for this meeting, we send copies of the new drafts to each group member, and ask that they read the drafts in advance and come prepared to provide input. We also assign one person from each group to write comments using the case review form, and ask that person to lead off the small group discussion. Most participants find these discussions very rich.

During the large group part of the meeting, we discuss such pertinent issues as deadlines for final drafts, confidentiality for people and places in the cases, use of pseudonyms, and authorship. The latter can be a delicate topic. Some people want very much to have their names associated with their case. Others prefer anonymity, if they fear confidentiality for persons in their narrative is at risk. Our rule of thumb is: If one person is concerned about confidentiality, all narratives will be anonymous and case writers will be recognized in a list of contributors.

Final drafts. The writers make their final revisions based on feedback from the meeting and, possibly, ongoing e-mail or phone conversations with the editors. When we receive the final drafts, the editors examine them once again. Are the cases compelling? Are the teachers' dilemmas clear? Will the cases stimulate analysis and rich discussion? Usually we are pleased with the drafts and set them aside. But occasionally we still have questions and make these queries by phone. Usually we'll make these changes to the text and send the final narrative to the author for approval. When all of the narratives meet our final draft criteria, we enter the last stage of the process. This entails sending the cases to an outside editor and returning them to the authors with the editor's notations and questions. Sometimes the authors make final changes; sometimes we make them at their request. Authors always have the final word on suggested revisions.

Celebration time. When all of the cases are completed, we compile them into a draft casebook, make a copy for each author, and gather once again for a final meeting. This is a time of celebration, with good food and reminiscences. It's also a time for final agreements about authorship. This group decided to have their names associated with their individual cases. We also use part of the celebration to engage them in a group reflection on this process. For this volume, we videotaped the discussion, transcribed the dialogue, and analyzed the impact of the writing process on their practice (see the section on "The Impact of Writing Cases" in the Preface).

Field Test

The field test represents the final step of the case development process. This is when we use the cases with other teachers to see what kind of discussion ensues. While one editor conducts the discussion, another takes notes. Often these sessions are tape-recorded for further reference. The field test has two purposes. First, we use a transcript of the case discussion as grist for developing the teaching notes in the facilitator's guide that accompanies each casebook. We are also interested to see if any parts of the discussion appear to be problematic and could be resolved by a simple addition to the text. For example, in one case discussion participants wondered whether a particular fluency assessment was given in English or Spanish, and raised some questions about the dynamics of the particular bilingual immersion school described in the text. This part of the discussion went off track and didn't seem to be productive to the teachers, as we learned during the debrief of the discussion afterwards. So we added some additional information to the text that forestalled such questions.

Facilitator's Guide

When the field test is complete, the editors compile the data from the field test and develop teaching notes for each case. These notes, together with an introduction to case discussion methods, are incorporated in a facilitator's guide to the casebook. In our experience, these materials are very important for new and veteran discussion leaders who want to use the cases in their own programs. The notes analyze key issues and offer sample probing questions that facilitators can use in their own discussions. They may also present additional background material on some of the challenges raised by the case writers.

SUMMARY

This methodological note described the process of developing *Using Assessments in Teaching for Understanding*. We focused primarily on our methods of guiding authors to progress from creating case seeds to crafting teaching cases. The development process was both time-consuming and rigorous, with multiple opportunities for collegial input from the community of case writers and editors. We felt the need for this degree of rigor, given our goal to publish cases that were both authentic to the authors and powerful enough to stimulate rich analysis and discussion among others. Such rigor may not be necessary for groups that want to use case writing as a constructive tool to stimulate substantive discussion among students in a university course or within a community of practitioners. Indeed, the most important feature of our method is the creation of a safe and active teacher learning community. In that setting, individual experiences become shared narratives. These stories are then both interrogated and appreciated until they are transformed into teaching cases. They remain personal, but they emerge as "community property," a source of learning for all.

NOTES

1. Michele Lew, a staff developer who coordinated one of our collaborating teacher networks, was asked to be an editor a bit later on in the project.

2. This two-day seminar can be used as an excellent professional development activity for educators who want to grapple with pertinent issues through lively discussion/dialogue, whether or not their narratives will end up as published cases. I have used the same seminar structure to work with principals and beginning teachers who had no interest in ultimately publishing their work.

REFERENCES

Shulman, J. H. (1991). Revealing the mysteries of teacher-written cases: Opening the black box. *Journal of Teacher Education, 42*(4), 250–262.

Shulman, J. H., with Kepner, D. (1999). The editorial imperative: Responding to productive tensions between case writing and individual development. *Teacher Education Quarterly, 26*(1), 91–111.

APPENDIX A

Guidelines for Writing Cases

This casebook provides a way of capturing veteran teachers' knowledge about using multiple forms of assessment in diverse classrooms. The current push for standards-based instruction toward greater student understanding is strong. The challenge for teachers is to capture learning for understanding through appropriate assessment strategies and use that information to improve instruction. This casebook will offer accounts of teachers' experiences in designing and using such assessments.

What Do We Mean By a "Case?"

The cases we publish are original, teacher-written accounts that are crafted into teaching cases. These cases are not simply stories that a teacher might tell. They have several distinguishing features, such as:

- They are situated in an event or series of events that unfold over time.
- They have a plot that is problem-focused, with some dramatic tension that must be relieved.
- They are embedded with many problems that can be framed and analyzed from various perspectives.
- They include the thoughts and feelings of the teacher-writers as they render their accounts.
- And they include reflective comments that examine what the authors have learned from the experience and/or what they may do differently in another situation.

All stories are not cases. To call something a case is to make a theoretical claim that it is a "case of something" or an instance of a larger class (L. Shulman, 1986, p. 11). This is not to say that all cases illustrate, exemplify, or teach a theoretical principle. Cases are usually accounts of practical or strategic dilemmas that confront a teacher. To be valuable as a case, however, the narrative should be representative of a class or type of dilemma, problem, or quandary that arises with some frequency in teaching situations. Asking "What is this a case of?" is central to the collaborative inquiry with teacher-authors. We develop a shared understanding of what the case has taught the writer and could potentially teach others, and then identify which details of the story may be critical for understanding its meaning and those that are peripheral.

Writing a Case

A compelling case for this volume should be built around a problem that is puzzling for you and is probably common with many teachers. It's best to select a problem that wasn't easy to solve. You tried to resolve it with several alternatives before succeeding or giving up. Try to think of a classroom dilemma where questions can be raised about how best to approach it.

The most powerful cases are written with some dramatic quality, using all the elements of good narrative. The accounts are written so that readers will identify immediately with the teacher who confronts the problem and will want to know what happened. Don't worry about the quality of your writing in the first draft. You will have opportunities to revise and polish. Editing will also be done before a case is published.

Structure of a Case

First, describe your problem, identifying who you are. Next, provide some context (type of school, students, community). Then write as vivid an account as you can. What was your plan of action? What did you think would happen? What actually happened? Specifically indicate if or when the cultural or ethnic background of students (and

128   Appendix A

language) played an important part in your teaching intervention or practice. At the end, reflect on what happened in your case and incorporate any questions that could stimulate analysis and discussion of your situation.

TOPICS TO CONSIDER

This case initiative focuses on the challenges and dilemmas associated with *assessing* student learning. *Assessment* involves a variety of activities and functions. They include: 1) determining what students should know and be able to do; 2) designing, using, and interpreting assessments that are faithful to those outcomes; 3) incorporating assessments into instruction; 4) using those tools and outcomes as the basis for communicating, reporting, and making grading decisions; 5) involving students as responsible parties in self-assessment and the monitoring of their own learning; and 6) using assessments and their outcomes beyond the classroom context.

1. *Determining what students should know and be able to do.* These cases should focus on the curricular challenges of using standards (developed by your school, district, or state) in creating units of instruction and related assessment tasks, tailored to the needs of your students. How do you determine the desired outcomes, their relative priorities, and their compatibility with local, district, state, or national standards?
2. *Designing, using, and interpreting assessments that capture student learning.* This category includes such issues as creating appropriate assessment tools; developing benchmarks, rubrics, exemplars, and scoring guides; using student work as data and/or evidence of student learning; and deciding next steps for teaching.

3. *Incorporating assessments into instruction.* These cases deal with concerns voiced by some teachers that "authentic" assessments take too much time away from instruction. How do you deal with these concerns? How can you integrate assessment into instruction so that the assessment doesn't "come at the expense of instructional time"?
4. *Using assessment tools for reporting and grading.* Issues in this category include how to use a variety of assessment sources for grading, how to incorporate alternative or performance assessment data in a report card, how to report student progress to parents and other audiences, and how to balance accountability expectations with day-to-day assessments of student progress.
5. *Involving students in their self-assessment and learning.* These cases deal with the challenges of engaging all students in the process of taking responsibility for their own learning. Issues may include setting goals and expectations for learning, engaging in dialogue with peers about learning, and using standards and assessment data to improve their work.
6. *Using assessments and their outcomes beyond the classroom.* Many colleagues and stakeholders are intensely interested in the assessment of educational outcomes. These include administrators, parents, board members, policymakers, journalists, and members of the general public. Issues here include the complexities of talking about assessment to these professional and public constituencies and the consequences of such conversations and debates.

REFERENCE

Shulman, L. S. (1986). Those who understand: Knowledge growth in teaching. *Educational Researcher, 15*(2), 4–14.

Interstate New Teacher Assessment and Support Consortium (INTASC) Model Standards for Beginning Teacher Licensing and Development

1. The teacher understands the central concepts, tools of inquiry, and structures of the discipline(s) he or she teaches and can create learning experiences that make these aspects of subject matter meaningful for students:
   - Uses multiple representations
   - Uses differing viewpoints, theories, "ways of knowing," and methods of inquiry

2. The teacher understands how children learn and develop, and can provide learning experiences that support their intellectual, social, and personal development:
   - Assesses individual and group performance in all domains
   - Stimulates student reflection on prior knowledge, links new ideas to familiar ideas, makes connections to student experience, provides opportunities for active engagement, manipulating and testing of ideas, encourages students to assume responsibility for shaping their learning tasks

3. The teacher understands how students differ in their approaches to learning and creates instructional opportunities that are adapted to diverse learners:
   - Identifies and designs instruction appropriate to students' stages of development
   - Uses teaching approaches that are sensitive to the multiple experiences of learners and that address different learning and performance modes
   - Makes appropriate provisions for individual students (in terms of time and circumstances for work, tasks assigned, communication and response modes) for individual students who have particular learning differences or needs

   - Can identify when and how to access appropriate services or resources to meet exceptional needs
   - Seeks to understand students' families, cultures, and communities, and uses this information as a basis for connecting instruction to students' experiences
   - Brings multiple perspectives to the discussion of subject matter, including attention to students' personal, family, and community experiences and cultural norms
   - Creates a learning community in which individual differences are respected

4. The teacher understands and uses a variety of instructional strategies to encourage students' development of critical thinking, problem-solving, and performance skills:
   - Carefully evaluates how to achieve learning goals, choosing strategies and materials to achieve different instructional purposes and to meet student needs
   - Uses multiple teaching and learning strategies to engage students in active learning opportunities that promote development of critical thinking, problem solving, and performance capabilities that help students assume responsibility for identifying and using learning resources
   - Constantly monitors and adjusts strategies in response to learner feedback
   - Varies his or her role in the instructional process (instructor, facilitator, coach, audience) in relation to the content and purposes of instruction and the needs of students
   - Develops a variety of clear, accurate presentations and representations of concepts, using alternative explanations to assist stu-

dents' understanding and presenting diverse perspectives to encourage critical thinking

5. The teacher uses an understanding of individual and group motivation and behavior to create a learning environment that encourages positive social interaction, active engagement in learning, and self-motivation:

- Creates a smoothly functioning learning community in which students assume responsibility for themselves and one another, participate in decision making, work collaboratively and independently, and engage in purposeful learning activities
- Engages students in individual and cooperative learning activities that help them to develop the motivation to achieve
- Organizes, allocates, and manages the resources of time, space, activities, and attention to provide active and equitable engagement of students in productive tasks
- Maximizes class time spent in learning by creating expectations and processes of communication and behavior along with a physical setting conducive to classroom goals
- Helps group to develop shared values and expectations for student interactions—individual and group responsibility that create a positive classroom climate of openness, mutual respect, support, and inquiry
- Organizes, prepare students for, and monitors independent and group work that allows for full and varied participation of all individuals

6. The teacher uses knowledge of effective verbal, nonverbal, and media communication techniques to foster active inquiry, collaboration, and supportive interaction in the classroom:

- Models effective communication strategies in conveying ideas and in asking questions (e.g., monitoring the effects of messages, restating ideas, being sensitive to nonverbal cues)
- Supports and expands learner expression in speaking, writing, and other media
- Knows how to ask questions and stimulate discussion in different ways for particular purposes—probing for learner understanding, helping students articulate ideas.

- Communicates in ways that demonstrate a sensitivity to cultural and gender differences (appropriate use of eye contact, interpretation of body language, responsiveness to different modes of communication and participation)
- Knows how to use a variety of media communication tools, including audiovisual aids and computers, to enrich learning opportunities

7. The teacher plans instruction based upon knowledge of subject matter, students, the community, and curriculum goals:

- Plans for learning opportunities that recognize and address variation in learning styles and performance modes
- Creates lessons and activities that operate multiple levels to meet the developmental and individual needs of diverse learners and help each progress
- Creates short- and long-term plans that are linked to student needs and performance, and adapts plans to ensure and capitalize on student progress and motivation
- Responds to unanticipated sources of input, evaluates plans in relation to short- and long-range goals, and systematically adjusts plans to meet student needs and enhance learning

8. The teacher understands and uses formal and informal assessment strategies to evaluate and ensure the continuous intellectual social and physical development of the learner:

- Uses a variety of formal and informal assessment techniques (observation, portfolios of student work, student-made tests, performance tasks, projects, students' self-assessments, peer assessments, and standardized tests) to enhance students' performance, and modify teaching and learning strategies
- Teacher solicits and uses information about students' experiences, learning behavior, needs, and progress from parents, other colleagues, and students themselves
- Teacher uses assessment strategies to involve learners in self-assessment activities, to help them become aware of their strengths and needs, and to encourage them to set personal goals for learning

- Evaluates effect of class activities on both individuals and class as a whole, collecting information through observation of classroom interactions, questioning, and analysis of student work
- Monitors his or her own teaching strategies and behavior in relation to student success, modifying plans and instructional approaches accordingly
- Maintains useful records of student work and performance and can communicate student progress knowledgeably and responsibly, based on appropriate indicators, to students, parents, and other colleagues

9. The teacher is a reflective practitioner who continually evaluates the effects of his choices and actions on others (students, parents, and other professionals in the learning community) and who actively seeks out opportunities to grow professionally:
   - Uses classroom observation, information about students, and research as sources for evaluating the outcomes of teaching and learning and as a basis for experimenting with, reflecting on, and revising practice
   - Seeks out professional literature, colleagues, and other resources to support his/her own development as a learner and a teacher
   - Draws upon professional colleagues within the school and other professional arenas

as supports for reflection, problem-solving, and new ideas, actively sharing experiences and seeking and giving feedback

10. The teacher fosters relationships with school colleagues, parents, and agencies in the larger community to support students' learning and well-being:
    - Participates in collegial activities designed to make entire school a productive learning community
    - Makes links with the learners' other environments on behalf of students, by consulting with parents, counselors, teachers of other classes and activities within schools, and professionals in other community agencies
    - Can identify and use community resources to foster student learning
    - Establishes respectful and productive relationships with parents and guardians from diverse home and community situations, and seeks to develop cooperative partnerships in support of student learning and well being
    - Talks with and listens to the student, is sensitive and responsive to clues of distress, investigates situations and seeks outside help as needed and appropriate to remedy problems
    - Acts as an advocate for students

The above list is paraphrased from the INTASC standards, it is not quoted verbatim.

Annotated Bibliography

TENSIONS BETWEEN ACCOUNTABILITY AND STUDENT LEARNING

Barton, Paul E. (1999). *Too much testing of the wrong kind: Too little of the right kind in K–12 education.* Princeton, NJ: Educational Testing Service.

This report begins with a brief review of standardized testing in schools, and the reasons for the growing reliance on testing to evaluate the effectiveness of our educational system. Barton summarizes the new trends in testing and highlights the tensions between accountability and assessing student learning. He states that the purpose of standardized testing is to provide teachers, administrators, policymakers, and the public with better information to improve classroom instruction and student achievement. However, current testing measures fail to provide the information that will actually result in changes within schools. Sample-based approaches (e.g., NAEP assessments) provide better information about schools, are much less intrusive into instructional settings, and require less frequent testing. Barton describes the proposal for a voluntary national test and the potential consequences of this assessment. An alternative assessment technique, the "patient approach," which focuses on setting content standards and aligning curriculum and assessment techniques to the standards, is discussed. The report also addresses the challenges of setting performance standards as well as exit examinations. Finally, he explains the critical role of the teacher in assessing students and the importance of professional development to equip teachers with the knowledge and tools to use assessments in daily classroom instruction.

McColskey, Wendy, & McMunn, Nancy. (2000, October). Strategies for dealing with high-stakes state tests. *Phi Delta Kappan*, 115–120.

This article addresses the dilemma teachers face between improving test scores quickly and focusing on strategies that support high quality learning environments in all classrooms. The impact of high-stakes tests and accountability policies that have both positive and unintended negative consequences are discussed. The authors state that many districts institute short-term strategies to increase test scores but neglect to examine whether these strategies will enhance student motivation, learning, and development over time. A brief description of two school models is included: one focused on quick fixes to increase test scores is contrasted with another focused on long-term strategies for improving student achievement. The article urges district and school leaders to include teachers in the planning of specific test preparation strategies and to develop a reasonable set of educationally defensible strategies that will have a positive long-term impact on student learning.

Nave, Bill; Miech, Edward; & Mosteller, Frederick. (2000, October). A lapse in standards: Linking standards-based reform with student achievement. *Phi Delta Kappan*, 128–132.

There is little empirical evidence that supports or refutes the existence of a causal link between standards and enhanced student learning. In this article, the authors critique five "theories of action," discuss a study that proposes a concrete mechanism, and present two small case studies that suggest how standards can affect student learning in daily practice. The authors differentiate between three types of standards: content, performance, and opportunity-to-learn. Advocates of standards-based reform might subscribe to one or more of five theories of action: 1) use ambitious, uniform expectations to inspire students to achieve at higher levels; 2) use ambitious, uniform expectations to inspire teachers to believe that their students can achieve at higher levels; 3) use a big stick to wake up and challenge unmotivated students; 4) use a big stick to wake up and challenge unmotivated teachers; and 5) use a collaborative process when setting standards to increase stakeholder investment in improving teaching and learning. Hornbeck's theory of action, implemented in the Philadelphia School District, includes: 1) hold high expectations for all students; 2) create content and performance standards that apply to all students and create a K–12 curriculum guide based on those standards; 3) place the curriculum guide in the hands of teachers and provide professional development time for them to become familiar with its content; 4) expect teachers to incorporate the guide into their lesson planning; 5) expect students to learn more from these new lessons and classroom experiences; 6) expect these students to perform better on the district's standardized tests; and 7) hold principals accountable for classroom-by-classroom improvements in student achievement. Finally, the authors examine two small case studies that support the use of standards to improve student achievement.

Ohanian, Susan. (1999). *One size fits few: The folly of educational standards*. Portsmouth, NH: Heinemann.

In this book, Ohanian questions our national reliance on standards and discusses the implications of allowing standards to dictate the instructional practices in classrooms. Ohanian claims that a one-size-fits-all curriculum ends up fitting nobody. She explains the fallacy of assuming that the college prep curriculum provides a quality education for all students. She urges educators at all levels to focus on the needs of individual students. Numerous examples of how standards-based curricula are failing to meet the needs of students are presented throughout the book. She describes cases where teachers determine students' prior knowledge and interests and customize instruction to assist the students in reaching their maximum potential.

Popham, W. James. (1999). Where large scale educational assessment is heading and why it shouldn't. *Educational Measurement, 18*(3), 13–17.

In this article, the key question is, "Why does instructional enhancement take a back seat to educational accountability?" Popham defines instructional enhancement as improving the quality of the educational experience provided to students. Educational accountability is defined as accumulating evidence to help determine if educational expenditures (both of energy and of money) are achieving their intended consequences. The article focuses on the reasons for the imbalance between accountability and instruction when the emphasis is on accountability. The overwhelming emphasis on accountability has resulted in a lack of focus on the primary mission of education, namely, teaching students what they need to know and do. He states that instructional enhancement must be viewed as an equivalent partner along with accountability. To accomplish this balance, Popham recommends: test development groups containing people who understand the instructional implications of what is being measured in the assessment; selection of skills to be assessed that are instructionally useful as well as valid assessment measures; identification of the entire knowledge domain to be assessed prior to developing a specific test item; and realization that nationally standardized achievement tests should not be used as the only measure to evaluate educational quality.

Wiggins, Grant P. (1993). *Assessing student performance: Exploring the purpose and limits of testing*. San Francisco: Jossey-Bass.

In this book, Grant Wiggins distinguishes between the terms *assessment* and *testing*. "An assessment is a comprehensive, multifaceted analysis of performance: it must be judgement-based and personal. An educational test, by contrast, is an 'instrument,' a measuring device." He describes his rationale for authentic assessment and explains why assessment should be a method for improving student performance, not just a mechanism for measuring it. Wiggins encourages the reader to consider what testing would look like if the primary focus was on improving students' intellectual accomplishments and not a device for measuring the effectiveness of the teacher and/or school. He asks questions that strike at the heart of the current evaluation system, such as: "What do we mean by *mastery*? What justifications exist for how we grade the way we do? How can unrelenting secrecy in testing be justified?" Wiggins explores the problematic practices in testing procedures that are widely used today, such as secrecy, answer distracters, scoring systems, and test formats that do not provide students with opportunities to explain their answers. Throughout the book, Wiggins provides examples of assessments that are intended to increase students' learning and promote deeper understanding. He encourages the use of incentives and concurrent specific feedback to enable students to make intelligent adjustments to their performance instead of receiving feedback that simply tells learners whether their answers are right or wrong at the end of the testing period.

DESIGNING, USING, AND INTERPRETING ASSESSMENTS THAT CAPTURE STUDENT LEARNING

Campbell, Dorothy M.; Melenyzer, Beverly J.; Nettles, Diane H.; & Wyman, Richard M. Jr. (1999). *Portfolio and performance assessment in teacher education*. Needham Heights, MA: Allyn & Bacon.

The authors of this detailed book provide useful strategies to guide readers through the process of implementing portfolio assessments in teacher education programs. The primary audience for the book is teacher educators, for whom the book realistically portrays the conceptual and practical issues required to develop ongoing and meaningful portfolio-based instruction and assessments. The authors have built their portfolio approach around current educational practice and focus, including a constructivist philosophy, specified standards to guide instruction and assessment, and rubrics to assess student performance. The text does not seek to prescribe an assessment program for educators to emulate; rather, the authors furnish suggestions and examples that educators can realistically employ in their own classes. The first chapter starts with a description of two key elements required to structure and develop meaningful portfolio and performance assessments: a philosophy and standards. The authors provide useful questions to help focus students on the important features of the program. For example, questions such as "Why are standards necessary?" and "What would achievement of each standard look like in actual behavior?" are posed. The book includes two domains of assessment: student-based assessment and program-based assessment. Student-based assessment is described in Chapters 2, 3, and 4, which focus on the guidelines for portfolio development; checkpoints for ensuring the quality of student learning through the performance assessment and rubrics; and supporting students as they document their learning. The program-based assessment is described in Chapters 5 and 6. The authors explain a variety of approaches that they have used to assess and improve the portfolio-based assessment.

Cole, Susan; Coffey, Janet; & Goldman, Shelly. (1999). Using assessments to improve equity in mathematics. *Educational Leadership*, 56(6), 56–58.

The authors present an assessment strategy for promoting equitable access using a project-based math curriculum called the Middle School Math through Applications Project (MMAP). MMAP was designed to encourage underserved students such as minorities and girls into higher mathematics by engaging students in design project learning. The assessment strategy asks students to continually and collaboratively respond to four questions: 1) What are we learning?; 2) What is quality work?; 3) To whom do we hold ourselves accountable?; and 4) How do we use assessment tools to learn

more? In this assessment technique, students not only share what they are learning with the whole class by making connections between the activities and specific math concepts, but they hold each other accountable for quality work and meeting externally defined standards. This is an example of teachers and students working together to define standards for learning, quality, accountability, and evaluation.

Newmann, Fred M.; Secada, Walter G.; & Wehlage, Gary G. (1995). *Guide to authentic instruction and assessment: Vision, standards, and scoring.* Madison: Wisconsin Center for Educational Research.

The Wisconsin Center for Educational Research has studied how school restructuring can promote authentic instruction and student performance. The authors present standards for authentic intellectual quality in three arenas of teaching practice: devising assessment tasks, planning lessons, and scoring student work. This guide is the result of analyzing materials collected from 130 teachers and 3,000 students in mathematics and social studies from 24 "restructured" elementary, middle, and high schools nationwide. The examples in the guide focus on mathematics and social studies, but the standards can be applied to other subjects as well. The guide begins with a rationale for the importance of students constructing knowledge through the use of disciplinary inquiry. A set of integrated standards for analyzing teaching, assessment practices, and student performance is described. Specific examples of teachers' lessons, teachers' assessment tasks, and student performance that exemplify the standards are included in the guide. The guide also provides specific rubrics and scoring rules for applying the standards in elementary, middle, and high schools.

Solano-Flores, Guillermo, & Shavelson, Richard J. (1997). Development of performance assessments in science: Conceptual, practical, and logistical issues. *Educational Measurement*, 16(3), 16–25.

The purpose of the article is to provide educators with conceptual tools and procedures that promote sound performance assessment practices. The authors specifically discuss and illustrate the need for science performance assessments and the challenges faced by researchers and teachers when they develop or use performance assessments in the classroom. A performance assessment contains three components: 1) a well-contextualized *task* that requires the student to use concrete materials to solve the problem; 2) a *response format* that captures the student's response to the task (e.g., record procedures used to solve problem, draw a graph, construct a table, write a conclusion); and 3) a *scoring system* to score the student's responses. Another key feature of science performance assessments is that the task should recreate the conditions in which scientists work and elicit the kind of thinking and reasoning used by scientists when they solve problems. The authors provide a specific framework for evaluating the dimensions of a task and illustrate how four existing science performance assessments are classified.

Wiggins, Grant P. (1998). *Educative assessment: Designing assessments to inform and improve student performance*. San Francisco: Jossey-Bass.

Wiggins makes the most convincing case yet that school-based assessment should focus on improving rather than auditing student learning. He argues for assessment activities that actually provide students with a learning experience. He shows how properly implemented performance-based assessments can help students to reach challenging performance targets, incorporate useful feedback, and progress toward excellence. This book provides design templates, flow charts, and authentic examples to assist teachers in developing effective performance tasks and scoring instruments as well as tools for judging student portfolios.

USING ASSESSMENTS TO GUIDE INSTRUCTION

Allen, David. (1998). *Assessing student learning: From grading to understanding*. New York: Teachers College Press.

This book is a collection of work from some of today's leading educators in the field of assessment. Each chapter focuses on a practical method for collaboratively examining student work, including writing samples, visual work, presentations, portfolios, and exhibitions. The approaches provide teachers with specific strategies for examining what students have learned as well as reflecting on how to support students' learning rather than relying on test scores and grades as measures of students' achievement.

Shepard, Lorrie, A. (2000). The role of assessment in a learning culture. *Educational Researcher, 29*(7), 4–14.

In this article, Lorrie Shepard focuses on classroom assessment. She encourages the use of assessments that not only match the subject matter standards, but are also an integrated component of instruction to support and enhance learning. She urges classroom teachers to work collaboratively to develop assessment strategies that will promote a learning culture as well as improving achievement. Shepard briefly discusses classroom practices (e.g., assessing prior knowledge; feedback strategies; transfer knowledge; peer and self-assessment; and the use of explicit criteria) that she argues will promote a learning culture. In addition to monitoring and promoting students' learning, Shepard argues that assessments should be a mechanism for helping teachers to examine, revise, and improve their teaching practice.

Wiggins, Grant P., & McTighe, Jay. (1998). *Understanding by design*. Alexandria, VA: Association for Supervision and Curriculum Development.

Linking curriculum and assessment is one of the most critical problems facing today's educators. This book provides an excellent framework and a clear set of design principles to guide teacher curriculum development. According to the "backward design" of lesson planning, designing lessons for understanding begins with identifying what students need to know and be able to do and to determine what evidence will indicate that they have learned it. After these key components are in place, then the focus shifts to how the students will learn the material. Throughout the book, the authors stress the importance of explicitly stating what students need to understand and what is meant by understanding. Each of the ten chapters guide the curriculum developer through the process, using examples and identifying possible misconception about the purpose of backward design. The last chapter puts the whole process together and provides the reader with a design template.

USING ASSESSMENTS AS TOOLS FOR REPORTING AND GRADING

Brookhart, Susan M. (1999). Teaching about communicating assessment results and grading. *Educational Measurement, 18*(1), 5–13.

This article focuses on methods for communicating the results of classroom assessments. The author identifies strategies for communicating classroom assessment results by assigning grades, using methods other than grades, and clarifying results of standardized tests. The validity of grades as a measure of a student's achievement depends upon the quality of the assessment information on which the grades are based and in part on the procedures used to determine the grade. For example, if the classroom assessment is of poor quality or incomplete, then the grade obtained from the assessment will be incomplete at best. This reinforces the importance of preparing sound classroom assessments that are aligned with sound instructional practices. Grading should involve combining multiple measures of different types of assessments in ways that honor the intended criteria for assessing the instructional unit and provide meaning to students. The author provides helpful guidelines for what teachers need to know about assigning grades. Methods for communicating classroom assessment results other than grades include portfolios, conferences, exhibits, and rubrics. The author provides detailed information and guidelines for teachers to use these alternative forms of communicating students' achievement. The last section of the article concentrates on the importance of teachers communicating the results of standardized tests to parents, students, and other educators. In an effort to clarify standardized test results, the author explains the concepts of *norm group* and *norm referencing* as well as differentiating between *status* and *growth measures*.

Colby, Susan A. (1999). Grading in a standards-based system. *Educational Leadership*, 56(6), 52–56.

This article presents a four-step process for developing a grading system to use to evaluate, record, and communicate students' progress in a standards-based system: 1) design a workable format; 2) define three types of codes—type of assessment, level of performance, and time period; 3) create a gradebook with easy access to each student's grade sheet; and 4) monitor and make adjustments to the system. Colby provides a number of specific examples of how to develop a grading system and explains the advantages of this system.

Davidson, Marcia, & Myhre, Oddmund. (2000). Measuring reading at grade level. *Educational Leadership*, 57(5), 25–28.

An elementary school district in the state of Washington instituted an assessment plan to evaluate students' reading progress from first to third grade. A timed oral reading fluency measure was used to determine the reading level of all students in grades one through three. The district used this information to establish district-level reading fluency norms and develop grade-level targets. The district decided to use the information as a tool for monitoring students' progress instead of as a means for separating students. Teachers reported that using oral reading fluency measures throughout the year helped them monitor students' progress and enabled them to provide vital information to students and parents.

Popham, W. James. (1997). What's wrong—and what's right—with rubrics. *Educational Leadership*, 55(2), 72–75.

According to Popham, the term *rubric* is a scoring guide to evaluate the quality of students' constructed responses, and it has three essential features: evaluative criteria, quality definitions, and a scoring strategy. Evaluative criteria help the assessor distinguish between acceptable and unacceptable features of the students' work, whereas the qualitative differences found in students' responses are assessed using the quality definitions of the rubric. The scoring strategy can be holistic (a single overall judgment of the quality) or analytic (a series of measures that evaluate specific aspects). The increased use of performance assessments that require scoring of students' responses has resulted in a movement to create and use rubrics to evaluate students' performance. Popham claims that many rubrics contain four flagrant flaws: 1) task-specific evaluation criteria; 2) excessively general evaluative criteria; 3) dysfunctional detail; and 4) equating the test of the skill with the skill itself. After illustrating examples of the common flaws of rubric design, Popham provides an example of a mathematical rubric that meets his criteria for an appropriately designed rubric.

USING ASSESSMENTS TO GUIDE SUPPORT FOR BEGINNING TEACHERS

Black, Paul J. (1998). *Testing: Friend or foe? Theory and practice of assessment and testing*. Bristol, PA: Falmer Press.

This practical guide for teachers is divided into three key components of assessment: history and cultural foundations of testing; the purpose of and teachers' role in assessment and testing; and a close examination of the practical issues for successfully developing assessments. Black urges teachers to focus on a coherent program in which curriculum, pedagogy, and assessment are restructured to maximize student learning. He examines a wide range of assessment strategies from fixed responses to performance assessments to evaluate students' learning. He describes the purpose, limitations, and benefits of each assessment approach.

Mehrens, William A.; Popham, W. James; & Ryan, Joseph M. (1998). How to prepare students for performance assessments. *Educational Measurement, 17*(1), 18–21.

In light of the current trend to use performance assessments as a means for measuring what students know and are able to do, the authors ask: "What are appropriate ways to prepare students for performance assessments?" This article discusses the teacher's dilemma between aligning the curriculum with the assessment technique and teaching to the test. The authors point out that the results of a performance assessment can be invalidated depending on how the teacher prepares students to complete the performance assessment. For example, if students are assessed on a specific higher order thinking skill, the results are meaningless if the teacher taught students to memorize the correct answers or performance prior to the assessment. The authors propose six guidelines for preparing students for performance assessments. First, define what you want to assess before you try to assess it. Second, do not provide students with guided practice on a task that is identical to the performance test task. Third, provide students with scaffolding to understand the performance assessment format. Fourth, identify the criteria for the assessment prior to the instructional planning of the unit. Teachers need to clearly communicate the assessment criteria to the students. Fifth, throughout the instructional process, should stress the transferability of the skills and knowledge assessed by performance tests. Finally, foster students' self-evaluation skills, since students know the criteria on which to evaluate their own performance.

About the Editors and the Case Authors

Judith H. Shulman is director of the Institute for Case Development at WestEd. Her research focuses on the development of cases and their impact on teacher learning, on the professional development of teachers, and on approaches to engaging in the scholarship of teaching on one's own practice. Her publications include *Case Methods in Teacher Education* (Teachers College Press), several co-edited casebooks and facilitators' guides, and numerous chapters and articles in professional journals such as *Educational Researcher, Teaching and Teacher Education,* and the *Journal of Teacher Education.* Shulman has conducted seminars on case methods throughout the United States and abroad, and advises educators on ways to use cases as professional development tools. She is currently involved in an initiative to support National Board Certification.

Andrea Whittaker is an Assistant Professor of Education at San José State University in the Division of Teacher Education, where she teaches courses in foundations, literacy, and assessment to preservice teachers in elementary and secondary credential programs. Dr. Whittaker uses case discussions and case writing as a form of inquiry with beginning and experienced teachers. Her research interests include the design and evaluation of professional development programs for educators, teacher inquiry, and educational equity in K–12 classrooms. She is currently engaged in several school/district and university partnerships designed to promote equitable educational outcomes for children from diverse backgrounds. With over ten years experience developing and critiquing standards and assessments for teachers and their K–12 students, her recent publications and presentations have examined the use and misuse of these tools within the policies and practices of professional development.

Michele Lew worked at Joint Venture: Silicon Valley Network, a regional non-profit organization, on teacher professional development issues. She was also the project manager for the Carnegie Academy for the Scholarship of Teaching and Learning (CASTL)—an advanced study center for outstanding K–12 teachers engaged in the study of their own classrooms—at the Carnegie Foundation for the Advancement of Teaching. Michele currently serves as the district director for Assembly member Joe Simitian, a member of the California State Legislature. She received her B.A. in economics from Yale University and a master's degree in public policy from the Kennedy School of Government at Harvard University.

ABOUT THE CASE AUTHORS[1]

Jean Babb teaches Grades 6–8 Language Arts in the Palo Alto Unified School District.

Wendy Baron is a Teacher Advisor at the New Teacher Center, University of California, Santa Cruz.

Christina Carmelich teaches Grade 5 Social Studies in the Oak Grove School District.

Marlo Chavez teaches Grades 6–8 Language Arts in the Live Oak Elementary School District.

Marge Collins teaches Grade 1 in the Palo Alto Unified School District.

---

1. These authors held the positions listed here at the time this book was written. In some cases, authors have since moved on to new positions

Pat Dawson teaches Grade 2 in the Palo Alto Unified School District.

Keely C. Floegel teaches Grade 3 in the Pajaro Valley Unified School District.

Kathleen Flowers teaches Grade 2 in the Pajaro Valley Unified School District.

Carol Glenn teaches Grades 7–8 Language Arts in the Live Oak Elementary School District.

Lori Helman is a Teacher Advisor at the New Teacher Center, University of California, Santa Cruz.

Ellen Moir is Executive Director of the New Teacher Center, University of California, Santa Cruz.

Kerrin Murphy teaches Grade 5 in the Pajaro Valley Unified School District.

Michelle Phillips teaches Math in Grades 6–8 in the Mill Valley Elementary School District.

Susan E. Schultz teaches High School Chemistry in the Sequoia Union School District.

Leslie Smith is a Teacher Advisor at the New Teacher Center, University of California, Santa Cruz.

Pam Spycher teaches Grade 1 in the Santa Cruz City Elementary School District.

Gwen Toevs teaches Grades 6–8 Language Arts in the Santa Cruz City High School District.